ROAD PLAYER
The Danny Diliberto Story

To Harry
Danny Di Liberto

Jerry Forsyth

BEBOB

HB Platin
206.999.6655(M)

ROAD PLAYER
The Danny Diliberto Story

By Jerry Forsyth

Published by: **Bebob Publishing**
P.O. Box 530411
Livonia, MI 48153

Copyright © 2005 by Jerry Forsyth

First Printing 2006

Printed in the United States of America

ISBN 1-887956-26-3

Cover Design by Bob Henning
Cover Photo by Jerry Forsyth

Publisher's Note

This work is based on the life of Danny Diliberto and all of the stories within it come from his memory and are based on his recollection. No effort whatsoever has been made to ascertain the factual basis of these stories. They are stories, and like all stories, have undoubtedly been enhanced and changed over time. Those looking for an absolutely factual detailing of these years must look elsewhere. All references, representations, or statements in this book about actual persons, living or dead, are solely the observations and opinions of Danny Diliberto. They do not represent the views or opinions of the author or the publisher.

Acknowledgements

No book is possible without the help of many people. All of the material in this book was provided by Danny Diliberto, whose memory is as impressive as his cueing skills. Danny, thank you for the stories. I also wish to thank those who supplied photos. Mike Shamos of the Billiard Archive, Diana Hoppe of Pool Pics, Conrad Burkman of the National Billiard News and, again, Danny Diliberto.

Thanks also for the editing assistance provided by Tom Shaw of _Pool & Billiard Magazine._ Tom made very valiant attempts at teaching me the proper use of the English language, all to no avail.

A very special thanks to my wife, Fran, who gave me time off from the farm work to compile these stories and track down the photos. She shouldered my burden as well as her own and gave me yet another reason to be joyful for our 39 years together. To steal a great line from a good friend, Nick Varner: "She's the best roll I ever got."

Jerry Forsyth

Introduction

We rarely see life-changing moments when they occur. It is only later that we can look back upon them and know that this or that is what caused our lives to take the turns toward ill or good. When Danny Diliberto set out from Buffalo on his first road trip all those years ago, he had no way of knowing that his life had been permanently altered. But that first trip to the Hustler's Jamboree would become the sextant for the remainder of his life.

This collection of road stories from the vibrant memory of Mr. Diliberto are a great glimpse into the lifestyle of those who choose to be modern-day Ronins; lone-wolf warriors with no master save themselves. There are highs beyond belief and lows that no one should suffer. From facing prison because of a roommate who pilfered motel towels to winning hundreds of thousands of dollars on a single gamble, this is a life story that is anything but boring.

Diliberto excelled in four sports, all of which begin with the letter 'B.' He has been a baseball player, a bowler, a boxer and a billiard player. Boxing was his first love, but one that did not return his favors. An excellent puncher, his own hands could not stand the power of his blows.

It was billiards that gave him greatest fame and the life described herein. Any devotee of the game will find this collection a fascinating look into the immediate past of the game. From Las Vegas to Hollywood to the smallest towns on the most distant highways, this is the life of the roadman. A gambler's tale told in his own words. Enjoy.

"For you—I'm always on call."

Danny Diliberto

Chapter One
THE DIE IS CAST

I have begun to wonder of late where my fate rounded that corner and I took up life on the road. My best guess is that it was somewhere on Highway 57 between Chicago and Johnston City. But I would never have been on that highway, would have never put my wheels on the road to Little Egypt and beyond, if it weren't for *Sports Illustrated.*

An article in their February 25, 1963 issue enveloped me, though to place all of the credit for my path there is out of place. I was shaped as much by my surroundings as anyone. Growing up in an Italian neighborhood of Buffalo, New York, you learned the things you needed to learn. How to manipulate your surroundings, to convince, coerce, and cajole. When you were unable to talk your way out of a fix, you fought your way out. You grew up cagey and tough. You learned the value of an edge.

There was a Spartan attitude to America made necessary by the very real Cold War, and we considered the military to be contemporary champions whose exploits were told time and again in comic books and dramatized on television and in the movies.

Most veterans didn't come home to parades, but when their neighbors found out that they had served, then suddenly the guy at the diner wouldn't take their coffee money and the filling station always checked their oil and water. The American psyche contained two fears in the fifties. Polio was crippling its children and was the plague that panicked swimming pools and schools. And the Great Red Menace hung over everyone. The fifties gave us both Stalin and Khrushchev, leaders fond of trading terrible threats with the U.S. Americans lived in the greatest period of promise we had ever known and in fear that it might all end tomorrow in the 'duck and cover' position of atomic homage.

Neighbors talked to one another. They would invite each other over and grill steaks and drink lemonade and talk about the war. One of my neighbors would pull up his trouser leg and show you where the machine gunner grazed him on Omaha. Another had spent two years as a Japanese POW and everything he told was scary. WWII set a lot of my perceptions. I grew up watching the black and white newsreels of the battles in the streets of Europe. My faith in my fellow man was tempered by the views of the pitiful souls emerging as skeletons from the camps like Bergen-Belsen and Auschwitz and the charred corpses of the Japanese in their hiding holes.

Brave men were everywhere; heroes commonplace. We had Douglas MacArthur and Jimmy Doolittle, Patton, Einstein and Edison and Dr. Jonas Salk. We had Eisenhower, Ernie Pyle and Audie Murphy. Fiction bristled with the Lone Ranger, Red Ryder and the Shadow and all of this was bathed in the comforting glow of our victorious forces.

Normalcy sort of crept in around the edges of all this. The fellow who ran the corner Deli would show you the tattoo that the Gestapo had put on his forearm, his camp number, and then he would note your order on a tally pad that would be settled at the end of the month or on payday. That was the credit card of the day.

Kids in America grew up expecting to be heroes, as heroic as the generation that raised them. So if you were in America, whatever you chose to do, you wanted to do it as a hero. You wanted to be the best and that was the only goal to own. Nobody ever considered settling for second place. Americans played to win. When real Americans were told "it's not whether you win or lose, its how you play the game," they knew it was a lie. Winning was big. Winning was all that mattered.

I was a young pool player and winning was all there was. In pool, if you're not winning, then you're not successful and you better go do something else quick. Pool is a game for winners only. Losers are just a by-product and they cycle themselves continually up and down the food chain, going down to pick up fresh cash from the lesser players and then swimming back up to play with the top feeders for a while and to leave the big guys enough cash to play one another.

That way you're never out of action. You may be keeping a lower profile for a while, until the tides lift your boat again, but something always comes along. Someone always swims up from below to see if he can join the club yet—the group that occupies the show table in every poolroom in America.

Two years before I hit the road it was 1961, and I was straight out of the Army. Before going in I had been a pretty fair player. When I was seventeen, I was knocking down four or five hundred a week playing the older guys. My reputation was good enough that when I got out of the service I was invited to play in the Buffalo City

Straight Pool Championships. This was pretty exciting stuff. As a west side player out of the Italian neighborhoods, I had heard of some of the downtown players like Joe Moran and John Beatty. These guys were so good that while one shot, the other one could eat lunch because there were that many balls that would be run. So I practiced a little, got in stroke, and won the Championship.

I still had no inspiration to become a pool player. It was just something I enjoyed doing to raise cash. But the next year, in 1962, I got invited to play in the State Tournament since I had won the City. I went to Syracuse and I won it as well. Two tournaments and two wins gave me a real winner's attitude. About the same time the movie "The Hustler" came out and I loved the romance of the road it inspired. Then I saw the article in Sports Illustrated, *Battle of the Hottest Sticks*. It captured all the sense of adventure and wander-lust I had in me and set me on the road to Johnston City. The draw-ings of characters with wild nicknames really reeled me in. The gods were in Johnson City. Names that every scuffler revered. Luther Lassiter, Danny Jones, Detroit Whitey and Cornbread Red.

There were sketches of all of the major characters at the Cue Club. "Youngblood" (James Brown, listed as Javanley Washington), Tugboat Whaley, Daddy Warbucks (Hubert Cokes), New York Fats (Rudolph Wanderone, who later changed his name to Minnesota Fats to capitalize on the movie), Squirrel (Marshall) Carpenter, Cow-boy Jimmy Moore, Iron Joe (Joe Proscita), Hayden Lingo, New York Blackie (A.F. Bonife), Wimpy (Luther) Lassiter, Detroit Whitey (Eddie Beauchene), Cornbread Red (Billy Burge), the Knoxville Bear (Eddie Taylor), Weenie Beanie (Bill Staton), Boston Shorty (Larry

Johnson), Handsome Danny (Danny Jones), Joey Spaeth, and Pots and Pans (Bernard Rogoff).

These were mysterious, dangerous guys leaning against the wall, clutching cues, or bent to the shot as an entire room of sweaters watched. There was round-the-clock gambling and all the best road players in the country showed up. The tournament was billed as a 14-player One Pocket tournament in 1961, but many more than that showed up for the action. Money changed hands in Nine Ball, and Straights and Banks as well. *Sports Illustrated* popularized an action Mecca in southern Illinois.

I had to get to that tournament. Inspired by my state title and my $400 first prize, I resolved to go the next fall to Johnston City. In the meantime, my win at the state tournament won me the honor of playing Willie Mosconi on his next trip to Buffalo to promote the Brunswick Billiard rooms. In my little Italian neighborhood, that was huge as both pool and boxing were real popular and Willie's dad owned a boxing gym. Willie boxed some as a young man as well as being the most famous pool player ever. He was the nuts. What a warm-up for Johnston City the match with Mosconi would be. I would be playing what many experts regarded as the best stick ever and that should be pretty good preparation for whatever would come my way with a gamble attached down in Little Egypt. (The Johnston City area was known as Little Egypt because of towns named Cairo and Thebes and because of the immoral lifestyle of gambling, moonshine and prostitution that thrived in the area.)

To get ready for Mosconi, I went downtown every day to Gerran's poolroom and played Joe Moran for two bucks a game. It was he I had dethroned in the city tournament and he was always eager to take another shot at me, especially with a little cash on the line. By playing him Straight Pool, I began to learn the finesse of the game. I had the innate ability to focus, to concentrate on the shot at hand and not be distracted. But in these games, watching how he moved around the table and how great his touch was, I learned the value of patience and how to stay cool under fire. A lot of pool is lost not to an opponent, but to one's own emotions.

Every day at two I'd walk into Gerran's and Moran would be there, already knocking balls around on the Sport Kings. He was a short little guy, balding, and always wore a suit and tie. He had a Rambow cue that he treated as if it were blown from crystal and he always played with a cigarette, in a holder, smoldering in his teeth. I never could figure out how he could play with that smoke coming up in his eyes, but he always did and it never seemed to bother him.

Moran played a conservative game of pool. Breaking two or three balls out of the rack at a time instead of opening up the pack, he rarely got himself into trouble. When he got into a situation not to his liking, he would study the table carefully before sticking me someplace with a safety where my chances for success were as bad as they could possibly be. With all the table time I ran up against Joe, by the time Mosconi got to town some months later, I was a much-improved player.

The morning of the day the man would walk into Gerran's to face me, I awoke confident and ready. With everyone's expectations of Mosconi so high, I really had nothing to lose. When I got to Gerran's, the place was mobbed. Crowds filled the stands to watch

THE DIE IS CAST

Mosconi coax the cue ball around, and the poolroom was standing room only for over an hour before our match was scheduled to begin. Mosconi had decided we would play a 200-point match. Tournament matches in those days were always to either 125 or 150 points, but Mosconi wanted a longer test to avoid the possibility of the local hotshot running out and winning.

Still, for a while the match ran closer than Mosconi wanted. I had him beat 156 to 141 and made a break shot that didn't turn out, so I played a pretty good safe. Mosconi was in a trap as there was no way to escape the safety.

Mosconi got up, looked at the table, and walked to the back of the room where Bill Mills (the owner of Gerran's) was standing. The contrast between them was comical. Sophisticated Willie with his regal mane of white hair, all tuxed out, stood over the bald head of Mills, whose coke bottle glasses would glint as he turned his head or nodded in response. They talked for a little while and then Mills came up to me and said, "Danny, no safeties." This came as a surprise, the great Mosconi pulling a move on me to avoid losing. But I knew he was the star, the one they had come to see, and so I choked back my dissent. After the referee reset the table to where it had been before my safety, I had to kick a three-rail shot and didn't make it. Willie ran 59 and out. The crowd was pleased, but Mosconi avoided my eyes as he took his bows.

Later that evening, Bill Mills invited Mosconi and me to dinner. Mosconi had just been paid a ton for that little match and he stalled until Mills picked up the tab. I think that might be Mosconi's greatest run: 1,748 times he stalled until someone else picked up the tab.

ROAD PLAYER

Shortly after that exhibition, I got invited to my first really big-time professional Straight Pool tournament. Held in Rochester, New York, it was to be ten of the best players in the world. Jimmy Caras would be there, and Jimmy Moore and Irving Crane. I was invited for the local draw. The tournament was in a room Crane played in, the Olympic Bowl, one of the poolroom and bowling alley combinations that were so popular during the middle of the twentieth century.

The event was called the U.S. Masters and it gave me my first taste of the weirdness that can occur at pro events. The finals came down to a match between Irving Crane and Joe Canton. At the end of the match, the score line showed that Crane needed one ball. He was in a position that offered up no shot, so he played a safety. Canton played a great shot to get out of the safety and ran 27 and out to win the tournament.

To this day, however, if you look in the record books they all say that Crane won the tournament. That's because at the end of the match, after both players had signed the score sheets, Crane was leaving the arena when a fan took him aside. "Irving," he said, "you didn't lose, you won. You didn't need that last ball. You were already out when you played the safety."

"Well," said Crane, "I'd hate to go home tonight thinking I really won this tournament." He had a lot of attorneys in his family, so he got one of them to intercede and had the prize money frozen. *Nobody* got paid. And many of us needed the money!

Time went by and the attorneys kept putting on the stall. Eventually, Canton was coerced into a replay of the final match that would determine the outcome of the tournament. The worst part was that

Crane demanded that it be a 300-point match, knowing that Canton could not keep up with him for that long a stretch. Crane won the match easily and Canton lost his title forever.

One of the high seeds in the tournament was Frank McGowan, a great player from Brooklyn, New York. He was maybe the slowest player on earth, but he was truly great and seeded number two to win the event. He was my first match.

This was a round-robin tournament, so everyone played everyone. I beat McGowan to get off to a great start and began to get the sense that I belonged, that I could be a champion. But this may have sparked my confidence to the point that I lost my edge, because I got slaughtered the rest of the tournament. My performance waned and I finished the tournament disappointed, feeling like a loser.

I hated that. Used to winning, I had been beaten badly and this didn't jive with my need to be great. But Johnston City was coming up, and Johnston City would change everything. It formed my way of thinking, my way of earning money and it set the rudder for my life. The first year I went there was 1963, the year that the format would change. No longer just One Pocket, it became an all-around tournament consisting of Nine Ball, One Pocket and Straight Pool.

Soon, fall came to New York. The foliage turned color and left the trees. It was time for me to test myself, to challenge the odds and define myself. Buffalo, my home since birth, now became a well of memories, a place to visit and reminisce. I knew when I left that the anchor of my life had been hoisted.

Chapter Two
DOWN TO LITTLE EGYPT

Within a few days I was driving west from Buffalo to Chicago on my way to the Hustler's Jamboree. I was so excited that I drove straight through to Chicago. I got there just after sunset and decided to go to a poolroom and stretch my wings. The thought had occurred that maybe I should watch some One Pocket, since I was not familiar with the game and it was the main money-mover in Johnston City. I knew of a room out past the loop on the second floor of one of the old brownstones. When I went in, I found two young guys playing on the front table and two older guys on the table just behind them.

I grabbed a menu and sat down at a table near the action to decide on dinner. I needed to quell the hunger without eating anything so heavy that I couldn't stave off sleep. There was still an abundance of highway in front of me. My food hadn't even had time to get to my table when one of the old guys on the second table grabbed his chest and fell out into the aisle, dead of a massive coronary. After his playing partner found no pulse and said he was dead, the two guys playing Nine Ball on the next table got up and resumed their game. They were walking all around the guy, even making a stance while straddling his corpse. They were just too involved in what they had going on to worry about a dead guy on the floor. They were careful not to step on the body, but they didn't quit. This was my first indication that pool players might be a little different. I stayed long enough to scarf down some soup and a sandwich, then got back in my car and headed south on Highway 57.

A few hours later, around 2 AM, I saw the sign by the highway: 'Welcome to Johnston City, home of the World All-Around Hustler's Championship.' Off the highway you could see the Show-Bar with a large lit sign announcing itself in the parking lot. Behind it was the Cue Club. I turned from the highway, headed up the ramp and made a right turn. I parked and walked across the gravel lot into the Cue Club to see if anyone was still kicking around at this hour.

You would have thought it was mid-afternoon. The place was packed, thick with cigarette smoke and buzzing flies. The room had one pool table in the center with homemade bleachers facing in from both sides of the room. Dead ahead was a small door in the far wall that led to the back room where there were three more tables and this was where the real action was happening. A small bar was doing a brisk business with scotch and soda as the tonic of choice. It was terribly crowded, but the alcohol and action buoyed every spirit in the room and the only ruckus came from laughter.

The first match I watched that night involved a little guy in a derby hat playing One Pocket. He was only about five feet tall and reminded me of Moran because he had a cigarette always dangling from an overstuffed lower lip. This was Boston Shorty, Larry Johnson. Because he was so short he had negotiated a rule with everyone that if he couldn't reach a shot, he could jump up on the table and shoot.

Things were really tight in the back room. There wasn't room for many spectators, so most of the time you had to be either matched up or in on the action in a big way to get through the door and admitted to the back. On the second floor was an apartment with a bed and a bath and this was where they carried Ronnie Allen later that week when he passed out playing Cornbread Red.

Later, the word that went around was that Ronnie was jarred by some of Cornbread's friends because they were playing a freeze-out. A freeze-out meant that you had to continue to play until all of the money was either won or lost. If you quit for any reason, you had to forfeit the bet. Word had it that some of Cornbread's boys had dropped a mickey on Ronnie so he couldn't continue and would have to give up the dough. The druggers figured that Ronnie, being known as a heavy drinker, would attract little attention when he passed out. But George Jansco saw that ruse from a mile away and negated the bet so that Ronnie was saved from an ugly loss. The Janscos were the law at the tournament. It was their place and their cash in the prize fund, so they made the rules and you either lived by them or you could leave.

Being a stranger to this crowd was a bit like being the new kid in school. You needed a connection to get involved with the goings-on, an introduction to the inner circle of movers and moneymen. I was just remaining low-key, looking around and scoping things out, when I saw a friend across the room.

Bunny Rogoff knew everybody and was known as "Pots & Pans" because he would sell them when things got thin on the road. Rogoff became my steer man and enabler. He would tell me who to play, what game to play, and he would help to get the games set up.

DOWN TO LITTLE EGYPT

We went to the back room and found Squirrel Carpenter, from Tuscaloosa, playing Joey Spaeth from Cincinnati. I had never seen gambling like this. They were playing One Pocket for $500 a game! Squirrel reminded me of Spike Jones. He looked just like him except there was no white in his eyes, only dark brown. That's why they called him Squirrel, but he preferred to claim that the nickname came from being able to crawl around the balls without moving them. Man, he could really play. Bunny called him "the best money player on earth." But there were plenty of horses willing to run against him. Cornbread Red had cash behind his cue, as did Shorty and Weenie-Beanie, and it seemed like Lassiter could whistle cash out of the walls, he could raise it so fast. As days went by I began to learn more and more about what was going on. I began to get comfortable with the scene.

The atmosphere was beautiful and crazy. The Janscos were always coming up with stuff to entertain the crowd. Sometimes on Tuesday, which was Ladies Night, they would put the players in a hobbyhorse contest. Where they got adult-sized hobbyhorses I don't know, but the things were deadly. If you didn't have your rocking motion just right they could throw you off and you could break your neck. But Tuesday nights would find the greatest pool players on earth lined up across the side of the dance floor at the Show-Bar waiting for the starting gun. Off they would go, rocking across the dance floor in hopes of crossing the finish line first. It was a hilarious scene. The winner would get a bottle of champagne and sometimes there would be a side bet or two that might even cause a blocker to be in the field whose job it was to slow down another horse by falling into them or running sideways.

Other times, George and Paulie would throw a limbo contest and these were so ridiculous, you couldn't hear the music over the laughter. Imagine a room full of inebriated locals, gamblers, pool players and their women, all holding wads of cash wagered on limbo, as a somewhat tipsy Luther Lassiter gyrated beneath the limbo bar. One night Paulie got up and showed off a very nice bottle of French Cabernet Sauvignon that he would award that evening as first prize.

I happened to be standing next to Cicero Murphy when Paulie held up the wine. Cicero, one of the greatest black players ever, started bragging that he was the nuts for this limbo stuff. "You white boys can't bend at the hip. That's why the ladies don't like ya. Danny, get your thirst ready, we'll be uncorking that bottle after I set the mark."

So Murphy danced to the limbo beat, looking good and smiling a confident smile and when he got to the head of the line, he told them to lower the bar. Paulie obeyed and lowered it a notch. Cicero danced up to the bar, bent backwards, and just kept going over. His head hit the floor so hard it sounded like someone had thrown a coconut down. He survived the knock with a bruise and a headache, but we didn't get any wine that night and I never saw Cicero in the limbo line again.

The Janscos arranged for Tom Cosmo to open the evening matches with his show. Cosmo was from New York and I had first seen him in the late 50's in Miami Beach where he was a nightclub performer. He was a great dancer and he sang as well, but his name would prove to be his legacy. As part of his act, he would put nine balls out on the table. The way he did it, so casual and all, it looked like he was just randomly putting the balls out on the table, but actually each ball was placed in exactly the same place every night.

Then he would be singing and dancing and telling jokes and all the while running this rack of Nine Ball. His clowning and singing distracted the crowds so most people didn't realize he was just hitting one easy stop shot after another. Your blind grandmother could have run those balls, but it looked good and became the touchstone for easy runs in Nine Ball. Today, whenever someone has a really easy table to run, we say he has a Cosmo and that's where the term originated, from Tom Cosmo in Johnston City. Cosmo actually was a pretty good Straight Pool player. He beat Jimmy Moore once that I know about. Jimmy had Cosmo down 124-17 in a race to 125 and Cosmo wound up beating him 125-124.

Cosmo was a clever guy. Before he would start his 'run,' he would grab a twenty from someone in the audience and put Jackson's face under the nine-ball. Then when he pocketed the nine at the end of his 'run,' he would pick up the twenty, grin, and put it in his pocket. The chump in the audience would never ask for it back because Cosmo acted like he had 'won' it by running the rack.

To begin his act, Cosmo would come out wearing a hat, a big fur coat, thick eyeglasses and gloves. He started with one-liners, pulling the gloves off of his hands as he spoke and the gloves just kept peeling off and piling up on the floor at his feet. The whole while those old vaudeville gloves were coming off, the jokes just poured forth and he had the whole place roaring. It was a great show and the audience loved him. Cosmo was like Mel Tillis. When he talked he would stammer, but he could sing like a bird.

Players would come from all over the country to get to Johnston City. Many never entered the tournaments. They just came for the back-room action and would float in and out of town as the event unfolded. Since it was in the middle of the country, they came from all directions and routes and all developed 'spots' to play on the way to pick up traveling money. At Johnston City, it was big business trading out the names of the spots and who to play. Anyone who knew a spot, could stop and know who to play, what they liked to play, what they would go off for, and any problems that might arise.

The descriptions of these spots and who to play were better than descriptions you could get from the FBI. Man, we took notes on these guys. I remember a bar in Anaheim. The guy there was named "square-headed Frank," and if you had that name and walked in, you could pick him out right away. There was no doubt. Then there was "Crooked-arm Jimmy." Again, easy to pick out of a crowd. In Oklahoma there was "Tangle-Eye." You'd be trying to make a game of pool with this guy and his eyes would be off to the side, so you knew it was him. It was amazing that this guy could make a ball, but he could really play. Buddy Hall said he couldn't play Tangle-Eye. "I get dizzy just trying to stay in his focus. He always has me leaning to one side real bad trying to catch that eye!"

The spots that were traded in Johnston City were spread across the country from coast to coast and it was very important to manage how you gave them out and to whom. You needed to do business without robbing your own bank. You didn't give out your best spot to the whole room; you just parceled them out here and there.

Some spots were pretty common knowledge. There was a guy in Lexington, Kentucky, named Don who owned a jewelry store and frequented a poolroom that closed at six every day. Don would play snooker on a nine-foot table for three or four hundred a game and that spot got given out a lot because you couldn't wear the guy out. You could send a new stick in there every day. Another Kentucky gold mine was a guy named Mike. He had inherited some big money and spent every day turning a large fortune into a smaller one.

Over the years, I have teamed up with at least a dozen players and gone on the road to either a spot that I worked well, or one of theirs. One of the guys I teamed up with was Steve Cook, a real good money player who looked like he didn't know which end of the cue to hold—he looked so innocent. I knew that if I could get him in front of Mike, we could score.

Steve Cook looked so timid that in any poolroom he walked into, there would be someone who would play him just off his looks. That little-kid look of his was one of the greatest hustles I ever saw. He moved slowly and was a real gentleman, but boy, he could play.

I saw Cook in Arlington one year at Jack N' Jill's and I started thinking that he would be perfect for that spot down in Kentucky. The way it worked was that the guy would play you until he was out of cash and then he would want to play on a check. Now, a check is something most pool players don't want to see. You never know if it is going to cash or not, because anybody can sign their name on a worthless piece of paper. But this guy's checks were good. He had never stiffed anyone, so it was okay to play on his check.

I also knew that Mike would raise the stakes every game. He thought he could shake you with the bet. But when he lost, no matter the amount, you got paid. So I took Steve down to Kentucky and on the way I gave him the whole drill, about how the guy would raise the stakes all the time and how he would run out of money and ask to play on a check.

But if I were to go into the poolroom, Mike would recognize me, so I was stuck outside. Now, this is as boring as a stakeout, waiting for your buddy to go in, throw the line, sink the hook and reel in the fish. Man, it can take hours. Anyways, this time I was out there from noon to past midnight, walking up and down the street, going in the little coffee shops and stores that were across the road.

A little after midnight, the room closed down and Steve came out and got in the car and said, "Well, it went just like you said. He raised the stakes all the time, and when he ran out of money, we played on his check. When it was all over I had won $800 cash and he owed me another $1,800."

I said, "That's great!"

Steve looked at me and said, "No, he didn't pay me."

"What do you mean he didn't pay you?"

"He told me he didn't have any more money and when I asked him for a check, he said he wasn't going to pay."

So I asked Steve what he said when the guy stiffed him. He said he turned to the guy and said, "Well, you go ahead and be that way." So the meekness that got him games, also got him (and me) not paid.

Johnston City was a great learning ground. Here were the best players in all of the games and you learned how to play, how to make games, and how to get into action. You were taught who to look for, what to say, when to ebb and when to flow. There was a lot of time to learn because you were there for a month. That's how all the camaraderie developed between these guys. We were stuck together for thirty days doing business with each other. If someone got busted and had to leave to find easier work, we would all chip in and give him a stake so he didn't leave town broke. The Janscos would always provide bus fare for anyone who needed it.

Abnormal behavior was easy to find in Illinois. Detroit Whitey (real name Ed Beauchene) was a road player who traveled the country playing pool in any room he could find and the lifestyle had made him treacherous. One day, he wanted to sell me a pool cue, as road players are often compelled to do when they get down on their luck. I had no grand aversion to playing the pawnbroker, so I agreed to take a look at the cue that he had stashed in the trunk of his car. When he opened the trunk, I couldn't help but notice that there was a tin cup and a pair of thick dark glasses in there. So I asked him about it. Whitey always traveled with this real nice German Shephard dog and he told me that whenever he got broke, he would put the glasses on and go into a town with the cup and the dog and stick the cup out long enough to get the stake for his next game. "Danny, I can grab a good stake roll in just a couple of hours." This was the backup plan from a guy who once broke all the heavies in Johnston City during a Ten Ball game when he ran nine straight racks. That's unheard of action, but he did it and busted everyone in the room.

Whitey was a swell enough guy most of the time, but he could turn on you real fast. He had a habit of not paying off; that got one of his dogs shot to death by an angry debt-holder and there were a number of folks he could count on to hurt him if they got the chance. One morning at the Cue Club, George Jansco asked me to drive Whitey to his hotel about six miles away in West Frankfurt. Whitey had been gambling and drinking all night and was drunk in the crowd and the noise was sharking an important game going on in the pit. I put him in the car and he started acting up. At first, he was just singing and it was kind of funny, because the dog was in the back seat howling along with the song. But then I joked that the dog was off-key and Whitey shoved his left foot on top of my right foot on the gas pedal and wouldn't let up. I couldn't get the gas pedal off the floor and the car was accelerating fast and it got uncomfortable pretty quick. When the dog saw me struggling with Whitey, he edged up between the seats with his teeth bared and started growling real low and serious while the speedometer needle was bouncing back and forth across the gauge.

Finally, I turned the key off and the car started backfiring so loud it sounded like cannons. This was good as it made the dog spin around and look out the back to see about the noise. When the car lurched to a stop I got out, went around to the passenger side, opened the door and threw Whitey out of the car. Then I opened the rear door and the dog busied himself with sniffing his very drunk master to see if he was all right. I turned the car around and went back to Johnston City. The last I saw of Whitey that day, he was lying on the side of the road with the dog licking his face. The next time I saw him, the alcohol had dimmed any memory of the incident, or at least he never cared to mention it to me.

The promoters of the Hustler's Tournaments were two brothers, George and Paulie Jansco. Paulie was a tall fellow, while George was short and built like a tree trunk. George was the brain and Paulie was the mouth of the pair. The story was that they got their start in the 40's in Norfolk, Virginia. Supposedly, there was a man named Salinas who lived in Norfolk and was the boss of the numbers racket. He loved to gamble at pool and he was a big sucker. He played every pool hustler of the era and many of them left town wealthy. The Janscos took their winnings from him and went home to Johnston City. They bought the Show-Bar, a local pub, and converted a garage behind it into the Cue Club, putting an apartment and bathroom upstairs and converting the downstairs into a little two-room club. In 1961, Connecticut Johnny Vives won their first tournament, a contest limited to One Pocket.

Minnesota Fats had been instrumental in convincing the Janscos to throw their shindig. He and Hubert Cokes (known as Daddy Warbucks) made a convincing argument, and both men played important roles in the formative years of the event. Fats would entertain the crowds with trick shots and his usual line of absurdities and Cokes would create enough action to satisfy even the most hardened railbird. The first couple of years, the guys who showed up did so because Fats called them and they knew he'd keep talking until they promised to come. You knew that if you didn't show up, Fats would have a field day on your reputation and make up stories about you that would require years to dispel. When it came to Fatty, you didn't want to get into a pissing contest with a racehorse.

Fats only played in one of the events, preferring to make his way in the more familiar environs of the back room, where he could make the odds he needed to win. He was from nearby Dowell, Illinois, and came to many of the tournaments at the Cue Club just to be a showman. At that time, he was a very entertaining fellow who never shut up and held any room with story after story. Most of them centered around his being the greatest pool player who ever lived and how he had beaten all the Sheiks of Arabia and taken millions from the Maharajahs. According to him, he drove a car when he was two years old and left home when he was five because his mother asked him to take out the garbage and "they weren't getting me to do nothing like that." The entertainment value of Fats, however, soon wore off. After a while, you had heard all the stories and you were still supposed to laugh. His mouth, which had made him so many friends, began creating enemies.

Babe Cranfield got so tired of people asking if he could beat Fats, a guy who would not even play in most tournaments, that he made 1000 photocopies of the results of one where Fats took last place. Whenever someone asked if he could beat Fats, he would just hand them one of the photocopies; showing that everyone could beat Fats.

Cranfield was a bit of a character himself. When it was his turn to play, he wouldn't start shooting until all the chalks were lined up on the diamonds around the table. He would go around the table and look at each chalk and make sure it was placed correctly before he would shoot. On the break shot he would crouch down, put his finger on his forehead and stare at the break shot for almost a minute before he would stand to shoot.

There were so many characters in Johnston City. Hubert Cokes was one man who led a life dedicated to the road. The story was that he won an oil well in a poker game during the 20's and became wealthy from its output. He would come to the jamboree every year just for the gambling. He was a real nice guy whom you always treated with respect. When he was a young man, they said he was involved with a very pretty girl in some little town in the Midwest. The Sheriff there was hot on her as well and told Cokes to either be out of town by dawn or be ready to draw. They said Hubert faced the sheriff in a real old-style gunfight and out-drew the lawman, killing him dead on the spot. The jury acquitted him, saying it was nothing more than self-defense.

Hubert traveled with another pleasant fellow named Charlie. Charlie was one of those guys you just liked to be around. He had a quick smile and a great sense of humor. At the tournaments, while Hubert was down on the floor making the odds and writing out the betting slips, Charlie would be sitting and watching up in the stands with a .357 magnum under his jacket in a shoulder holster. He was under orders that if Hubert got into any trouble, to shoot first and figure stuff out later. Charlie had already killed two men that I knew of when I first met him, and he never voiced any remorse. That was just his job. When you won a bet with Hubert, you didn't go looking for your money. You sat there and waited to be paid.

But Hubert was a fair man. You didn't need to wet the chalk or anything when you played him. In fact, my very first week in Johnston City, it was Hubert who taught me the ins and outs of One Pocket. "You're here, so you might as well play in all the events." He showed me how to break to best advantage and then I drew him as my first opponent. The matches were to three games and I broke in the first game, made a ball, and ran out. Then he broke the next rack, failed to pocket a ball, and I got up and made a bank shot to get started and ran out again. Then I repeated the first game by breaking in a ball and running out. So Hubert only got one shot the entire set. He congratulated me and wished me success in the rest of my matches, never even showing me a frown.

Another road player who made the scene in Illinois was Alton Whitlow, known as "Babyface." He was an odd one, the kind of guy who would win matches he was supposed to lose. I was making the short walk from the Show-Bar to the Cue Club one night and I saw him wandering around out there looking lost. So I asked him if he was all right and he turned to me, obviously very drunk, and said "I got a match in fifteen minutes and I can't finds the door." So I showed him the door and he went in and shot the lights out and won his match. Ran ninety-some balls his first inning! Me, I could never make a ball unless I was sober, but some of the older guys wouldn't touch a cue without a buzz on. They claimed it took away the nerves and settled them down. Some guys showed up to play on uppers, 'snappers' as they were called, while others preferred a more calming medication. There were guys who carried a drugstore in the trunk of their car. They could provide anything you required.

Some real legends, the giants of the game, showed up in Illinois. Eddie Taylor, known as the Knoxville Bear, was well known long before he came to Johnston City. Eddie had a big round face, always smiling, and he and Harold Worst at the Show-Bar on ladies night would do an excellent soft-shoe dance together to the tune, "Walk through the Black Forest." Irving Crane came some years and Luther Lassiter came even during the four years he was Champion of the World.

Ronnie Allen was a regular attendee, as were Bill Incardona and U.J. Puckett, Danny Jones, Jimmy Reid and Bill Staton. Staton later parlayed his game and personality into appearances on "The Tonight Show" with Johnny Carson and the "Steve Allen Show." Ed Kelly would show up from Vegas and I drove in each year from Miami. Willie Mosconi never came. He was giving an exhibition only twenty miles away once, and someone in the crowd asked if he was going to go on down to Johnston City and "show them how to play." Willie replied that he would never attend an event designed around a bunch of two-bit hustlers. In truth, he simply never went anywhere that he wasn't the featured attraction or where he didn't have control.

The players thought that the promoters, the Janscos, were making a mint, but it wasn't so. I remember Joey Spaeth telling me once that George would steal your eyeballs and Paulie would say that you looked better without them anyway. Bitching about the Janscos finally had everyone convinced that they were having a bad time and just giving up money, but after it ended, we all missed it. For one thing, there were probably ten women for every man in Johnston City because the young miners, who had lived there once, had left town when the coal played out and left the women behind. The local women were not beauties. In fact, a story went around that there was a beauty pageant in town and nobody won. However, after the first week or so, those girls started to look pretty good. More than one player's wife had a dime dropped on her when one of the town ladies discovered their new lover was married.

I first met the colorful U.J. Puckett in the back room of the Show-Bar. Puckett was from Ft. Worth, Texas and he really was a Texan; big hat and boots included. One time the Janscos were trying to stake Irving Crane against Danny Jones playing all-around. Danny had a backer said to be good for around five grand. So the Janscos told U.J. that if he could set up the match between Crane and Jones he would 'get the pencil' at the bar all that night. 'Getting the pencil' meant that he would get free food and drink all night long, and a guy as big as Puckett could turn that into a pretty handsome jellyroll.

Puckett talked the deal up between the players and got the game turned on. It was no easy matter to pick a winner. Crane had a big advantage in Straight Pool, they were a toss-up at Nine Ball, and Danny had the edge in One Pocket. The way the match was designed they were to play Nine Ball first. Crane won that one and was looking pretty sunny, as the next game to be played was his forte, Straight Pool. Since they were playing all-around, comprised of matches in the three disciplines of the tournament, anyone who won two matches would win the bet. The match was over as soon as anyone won two of the disciplines.

As expected, Danny had no chance in Straights against Crane. Crane won easily and the Janscos collected their $5,000. And Puckett got the pencil he was promised. Being a mover, U.J. expanded the privilege he had been granted and invited me, Ronnie Allen, Ed Kelly and three or four others to have drinks 'on him' at the bar. We sat there with Puckett and drank all night long.

While we were drinking, Puckett told us a story. He said he was drift fishing one time by a dam on Lake Benbrook near his home in Texas. Drift fishing is when you have very little weight on your line and the current carries the bait and you hope it drifts in front of some hungry fish lurking near the bottom. Puckett said he got a big strike and after fighting it for a couple of minutes, the fish broke the line. So Puckett put on a heavier line and drifted his bait over the same area again. BAM! The same thing happened. He got the fish hooked, fought it for a few minutes, and the fish broke the line again.

Well, Puckett wasn't going to put up with some fish beating him at this game. So he got out the 100-lb. test line that is used for sharks and marlins, set his bait on the end of that, and floated it out again. As soon as he got over the same spot the fish hit his line for a third time and the battle was engaged. This time the line didn't break, but he couldn't bring the fish up either. He had been struggling with the monster for about twenty minutes when a boatload of divers pulled up. They were hired by the state to inspect the dam and do maintenance.

So Puckett, seeing these guys dressed out in wetsuits and scuba gear, yelled for them to come over as he struggled with the rod. They motored over and asked what the problem was. He told them he had this huge fish hooked, went through the whole story with them about the three strikes and all, and asked them to dive down and see what he had on the end of his line.

The divers all laughed, but one of them agreed and dove beneath the boat as Puckett continued to fight the fish. In a few minutes he surfaced and said, "You've got the biggest catfish I've ever seen hooked down there!" Puckett paused in the story telling, took a drink, and looked around to enjoy the eager ears waiting for the outcome. Then he continued. "But," the diver said, "there's a bus sunk down there and your fish has swam in and closed all the doors and windows!" The groans all around signaled Puckett that the suckers understood and he stood up, stretched, and left the bar.

Puckett was a big favorite among the spectators because he always put on such a good show for them. He and I played a great game of Straight Pool once and were both bantering with one another and the crowd and everyone was laughing and having a big time. I was teasing him about the U in his name standing for Ugly instead of Utley and he reminded the crowd that one time Fats had said I won the Florida State Championship by beating two Indians and an alligator.

The referee for this match was Norman Howard, nicknamed the Jockey because of his diminutive size. The Jockey was so much fun to watch that folks would stake him just to watch him play. As mentioned, Puckett was a great fellow, but he was also a very big man and his physical presence intimidated the Jockey. Things were going my way this day. I was beating U.J. by the score of 96-18 and was sitting in my chair wondering about his strange stroke. Whenever U.J. shot, at the end of his stroke the cue stick would go up in the air and way off to the left. He never stayed down on the shot like you're supposed to do. I never could figure out how he could play so well with that weird stroke. His stick went off so far to the left that anyone standing on that side of the table was subject to taking a cue tip in the face.

During this inning, I watched as Puckett got down on the six-ball and after he shot, his stick swooped left, but instead of coming up in the air as usual, it stayed down and hit some balls on the table, including the cue ball for a second time. The Jockey politely called, "Foul, Mr. Puckett." U.J. just kept on shooting like nothing had happened. The Jockey stood there perplexed and somewhat frightened. I went over to Norman and said, "Hey, what are you doing? He's shot four more balls after you called the foul and I want the table!"

Jockey promptly ran off to find the Janscos. He wasn't about to take on anyone the size of Puckett. Puckett was grinning and just kept on shooting. I sat back down in my chair, curious to see how this would be handled.

In a moment, George Jansco was looming over the end rail, demanding to know what had happened. Folks in the stands began to speak up since they had money wagered on the outcome, but George just raised his hand to silence them and looked at the Jockey. Norman said, "Mr. Puckett fouled and continued to shoot anyway."

George looked at Puckett. "U.J., sit your ass down! You fouled!"

U.J. raised his eyes. "Foul? It's a FOUL?" He took his cue stick and swept it back and forth across the table, scattering the balls everywhere and knocking some of them off to the floor. "Now THAT'S a FOUL!" he yelled, walking off. I was awarded the game and for the rest of the tournament, the Jockey walked around the block to avoid U.J.

Later, in the bar, U.J. came up and put his arm around me. "Danny, I knew I had fouled and all. I was just having a little fun. I didn't mean anything by it." Years later he met a fate that seems to be common among the road warriors. He got too old to play, and he didn't have any money saved from his years on the road. He wound up relying on the kindness of friends. They would take him around in a wheelchair to tournaments when he got real old and couldn't even recognize you anymore. But he knew voices. He would hear me speak to someone near him and he would reach out and say "Danny, is that you, Danny?" It was real sad to see. He was such a great guy, lived such a rich life, and had to wither away so slow. It frightened many of us to see U.J. like that. He was proof of the power of time.

The Show-Bar never closed. It was open 24 hours a day, seven days a week. It was always crowded with a mix of locals, players, small-time sweaters and big-time gamblers. Several characters, Daddy Warbucks for one, crossed the lines between player, stake horse and gambler. Warbucks shot a good enough game to finish in the top three a couple of years, so he could hold his own with a cue stick. But his real joy was in making nut games with guys who should beat him and then grabbing all their cash. Warbucks broke more guys than the depression.

Bill Staton was one of the real powerhouse sticks. He got stuck with the moniker of Weenie-Beanie because of the hot dog stands he owned in Alexandria, just outside of Washington, D.C. The story

DOWN TO LITTLE EGYPT

behind Bill was that prior to the hot dog stands, he was in another business and one of his employees failed to return from lunch. Bill went looking for him and, on a hunch, found him in a nearby poolroom. Bill somehow got into a pool game there, got hustled, and lost some money. The loss motivated him to take up the game, get very good at it, and to get revenge on the hustler.

Beanie says he is the only player to ever make a million-dollar score. He won forty grand in a game once, and didn't throw it back to the ponies, or a pit boss, or another player. He took the dough and bought his first hot dog stand outside of Washington. Over the years he earned well over a million dollars pushing franks through the window for a few dimes each. He parlayed that first stand into a chain around DC, that still funnels a handsome income his way years after he retired.

All of which is a pretty weird thing for a gambler to do. Gamblers don't usually waste money on bills, investments, or food. They keep it in flight. Every gambler is a bit tinged. Their logic turns in very narrow circles that ignore the larger planes of reality. Those who say it's not the money, just don't follow the line far enough. Of course it's the money. The money shows who is in the lead and who is trailing. So the logic turns on not surviving with money, but on how to best cycle it into larger and larger amounts. No score is enough. If you win hundreds, you are driven to turn that into thousands. If you win thousands, the demand is to create tens of thousands, then a million and then more.

The odds demand that you never get there, to that stage of wealth where you will say "that's enough." So when you hear tales of gamblers who won thousands and lost it back again, that is the basis of the logic. That it is never enough, never enough to quit. It would only be enough if it meant you never had to turn another card. Even those amounts are hard to hold by those who have the tireless need for action. Keith McCready once held over $120,000 in cash in his hands on a Friday night. On Sunday, I gave him three bucks for a hot dog and a coke. He had blown the whole roll in less than forty-eight hours. And that makes gambler's sense, because he could never have retired on just $120,000. That doesn't cut it. To be conservative and invest your funds at an average return of 3%, you need to have a million bucks just to generate an annual income of $30,000. So Keith needed to increase his score tenfold to retire even modestly, which wouldn't have been his style anyway. The man would need to win the mint. So, he's forced to keep the stake in action until the score is huge or he is broke.

Keith has maintained himself over the years, because his skills are such that not many players will take him down reliably. Others are less fortunate. In Detroit, a loser named Rosie would blow through six figures every week. He was the best example of an action junkie that I've ever seen. For him it was still the money, even though he was obscenely rich from his construction company, his government airfreight contract, and his bookmaking.

He wanted to go home with a bigger roll than he came in with, but he couldn't. He just didn't own the skills. He really couldn't make a ball. But he had tremendous wealth, and couldn't hang out with the Vanderbilts and their ilk because he was unable to hold up his end of any conversation. So he took up pool. He thought he could beat great pool players by jacking up the bet past their comfort level, while he remained within his. Everyone knew he was a loser, though, so he just kept on getting beat, week in and week out.

There was a group of about eight players that Rosie would rotate his action through and they did very well indeed. Rosie rarely made games well enough to enjoy the thrill of victory. He was so naïve that he never even knew his own moneyman was dumping him. The guy who brought Rosie in and handled the finances from their end was working with the players to set him up. This guy got half of everything paid out to the players beating Rosie. So Rosie's buddy was copping half the losses by acting like a trusted friend. The whole time he would support him and encourage him. "You're getting really good, Rosie. Your stick improves every week. Don't worry; you'll get him next time."

The bleeding of Rosie extended beyond the poolroom. He got dumped at everything. Even bowlers dumped on him. One guy he staked, one of the best bowlers in Detroit, once only needed seven pins in the final frame to win the bet. The guy threw the three-pin corner cluster on his first roll and then sent his second ball into the same, now vacant, spot. Rosie lost fifteen grand on that obviously crooked roll. Any other sucker would have pulled up right there. Instead, Rosie looked up at the other bowler's stake horse and said, "If you guys don't bet it up to thirty grand this time, I'm quitting". They won his money all weekend. The man would often lose over a million bucks in a single workout.

Chapter Three
FIST CITY

Pool had never been my first love. Even though it provided the medium for me to earn my daily bread, it remained a mere tool throughout my youth. My heart had always been in the ring. Boxing had been my design all along. My older brother Joey had been a boxer, a fact that traumatized my parents, and I was determined to follow in his footsteps and make a larger print. I would train under the great Angelo Dundee, the man who put the steel in a young Ali's (then Cassius Clay) fists.

It would never have been enough for me to match Joey's efforts. He had fought in the Golden Gloves and had knocked down Johnny Saxon, later the Welterweight Champion, before Saxon came back to stop him. He had gone pro briefly, residing in the same stable as Rocky Graziano, the one managed by Irving Cohen. But Joey got a cataract before he could polish his game and was washed out of the ring by the bad eye.

My fight pilgrimage to Miami came in the fall of 1957. I made my way to the gym that Dundee ran and demanded an opportunity to show my stuff. Impressed enough by my initial performance to give me a shot, Dundee assigned a trainer, George Roth-Seiden, to bring me up the fight chain. My parents thought that I had gone to Miami to avoid the Buffalo winter and work a normal job, so I changed my fighting name to Danny Toriani to prevent the sports page from becoming a source of concern for them.

FIST CITY

The mob was everywhere in the fight scene back then. Two heavies hung around the gym in Miami and lots of made men would come to watch the fights. The mob took a piece of everything that went on, a commission. They took part of the gate, part of the prizes, and part of everything. That's one reason fighters were paid so low, because so much of the money went to Italians with bulges under their coats.

You had to cooperate with those boys. They controlled the cards and if you weren't willing to go along you could be the best fighter ever and never get a shot at the title. They say that's what happened to Jake LaMotta. He wouldn't cooperate with them. He didn't think it was right that he would be out there in the ring, taking the risk of getting maimed or worse, and then having to share the profit with some character in a sharkskin suit.

So LaMotta went for years without ever getting a title shot. The rumor was that he finally realized the only way he would ever get the big fight was to go along with mob orders. They told him they would give him a chance at the title, but that he had to dump a fight for them first. He would be the favorite and they could clean up on the betting end of it.

Supposedly, he dumped a fight with Billy Fox and got caught. Billy, undefeated in over fifty fights, 'beat' the young and tough LaMotta. It was really just another clear message from the mob that fighters need to go along and keep quiet. If you raised a ruckus, things could happen.

Billy Fox couldn't fight a lick and he had never lost a bout. That's what the mob would do—build guys up like that by having all their opponents take dives. Some of them didn't even know that they were fighting dumpers; they thought they were winning when they couldn't really fight at all. All the mob had to do was to put them in against a fighter who wouldn't dump and they would get the 'upset' they needed to really clean up.

This was the world I went to enter. I drove down to Miami with a friend, Sonny, who was going there to look for work. He got a job as a bellhop at the Roney Plaza and we lived across the street at the Hotel Carib. My boxing career got off to a bad start. I broke my hand just weeks before leaving for Miami. I had been working construction in Buffalo. Well, not 'working' working. I spent most of my energy hiding from the foremen. The superintendent didn't even know I worked there. My family was connected to the trades, so I could get away with that stuff.

I didn't want the work, just the pay. I got paid one Friday and I was walking down the street window-shopping. I wanted to buy some clothes. I was looking in the windows at shirts and stuff and I accidentally bumped into a guy. "I'm so sorry!" I said. But he wouldn't accept the apology. He got huffy and sucker-punched me before I could react.

I couldn't believe it. I fell backward and when I got up, he came at me again and I nailed him with a right hand. I could hear the fourth and fifth metacarpals when they snapped. The punch finished him, but it may have hurt me worse. Once a bone breaks, it is easier for it to break in the future. During the ride south, I took the cast off of my hand and took the pin out in Jacksonville so that no one in Miami would know I was injured.

I wasn't going to be earning any fast money as a fighter, so to cut the nut, I delivered pizzas for Carmen's restaurant. Just across the street was Jake LaMotta's bar and the local mob used it as a watering hole.

I got no invitation to meet with Dundee. I hung around outside his gym until I saw him and went up and introduced myself. He asked me what I wanted. I told him, "I heard you're the best and I want to fight for you." He agreed to give me a chance. So my routine became delivering pizzas at night and working out during the day. As part of my pay, Carmen's would let me eat free. It was too hot to run during the day, so I waited and did my road work late at night when the heat of the sun was gone. I did all my running in Flamingo Park.

One of the owners of Carmen's was Johnny Peanuts. Every time Peanuts left town someone got murdered. But since Peanuts was out of town, they could never put anything on him. Everybody said he was a hit man and a mean one, but he gave me a job delivering pizzas and fed me, so I had no complaints with him.

Dundee watched me work a bag for a while and then put me with Roth-Seiden for training. George Roth-Seiden was also Dundee's partner. George and I evolved into very good friends and he became my mentor. After a while, he was like a second father to me. But the relationship didn't begin well. At first George wanted to throw me out of the gym. He had seen me favoring my shattered right hand, slapping the bag with it instead of punching and he didn't think I had the right potential. With the broken paw, I just couldn't deliver a great punch to the bag.

He kept me on the bags a long time. Every day I would beg Dundee. "Angelo, I don't want to hit bags. Let me spar! Let me show you what I can do." He kept saying "Danny, take your time. We'll get there, we'll get there." One morning, a little over a month later, Angelo was waiting for me outside when I came to the gym. "Let's go for a ride, Danny. Get in the car."

When I asked him where we were going he said, "I'm taking you to have a mouthpiece made." So we went to a dentist and had the cast made for my mouthpiece and then he took me to a sporting goods store and bought me a pair of sparring gloves. This was a set of 12 oz. gloves. Some guys would get the 16 oz gloves, the ones that look like pillows, but these were the 12's and were real serious gloves.

Finally I got to spar. Dundee put me with a pro boxer named Billy Ford. The first time we got into the ring together, I knocked him out in the first round. Ford and I had been sparring for only a minute or so, and I caught him flush on the chin with a right hand and he went down in a heap. Angelo was very impressed. Here I had never been in the ring against a live opponent before, and I knocked out an experienced fighter the first time I squared off against anyone.

After that I still harassed Dundee, but now it was for a fight. I felt I had shown my ability to perform and I wanted a chance to show it for real. "C'mon Angelo, you gotta let me fight!" His brother Chris was the promoter, the guy who actually arranged the fight cards, but Angelo would be my path to get to Chris.

Chris held his fights in the Miami Beach Auditorium. This was the same room from which the Jackie Gleason show originated. It was right next door to the convention center, where the big fights between heavyweight contenders and such were held.

My first fight was the evening of December 11, 1957. I was on the card for the Wednesday Night Fights. It wasn't originally intended that way. Another fighter had been scheduled. What happened was that on December 10, I was in the gym and I could see Angelo on the phone. He was nodding into the phone and looking around the gym and he saw me. "Danny, come here a minute." When I got over there, he held the phone down and asked. "Hey, do you want to fight in Tampa tomorrow night?" And I said, "Sure, you bet I do!"

At dawn the following morning, Roth-Seiden and I were to drive to Tampa in his station wagon. Angelo couldn't go. He had fights coming up in Europe with Carmen Basilio and Willy Pastrano. Basilio won the Welterweight title for Angelo and Pastrano, a light heavyweight, remained a top five contender his entire career. So the wagon to Tampa was filled with me, George, and two black fighters who were on the same card that night. We left at 5:30 in the morning. We had to be in Tampa for the weigh-in at noon.

I was scheduled to fight Tino Fuertes, an experienced pro who had never known a loss. At the weigh-in, I waited to see him for the first time. I weighed in at 137, skinny as a rail and I looked like a little kid. Fuertes weighed in at 155 and looked like a bull. The boxing commission had passed on this guy being a lightweight, but he outweighed me by over ten percent. When Fuertes and his manager saw me they looked at each other and grinned.

After the weigh-in, we went to our dressing room to rest for the fight. It was while resting in the dressing room, that I discovered that the worst thing about fighting is the waiting. There are other fights going on and you can hear the crowds yelling and the referee pounding the mat. One of the guys I had ridden in with, went out for his fight and got knocked out as I listened. All of us on the left side of the card were in one dressing room and the opponents were in the other. So when my guy got knocked out, they carried him back into our dressing room.

The other fellow I came with went out next and his fight got stopped on cuts. He came back in looking awful, blood everywhere. He had gashes on his face and a spurter above one eye. Meanwhile, as I was waiting for my fight, Willie Pep came into the dressing room. He said hello to everyone and when he saw my new face he came over to meet me. "Hey, kid, where ya' from?" When I told him Buffalo, New York, he said, "Oh, I fought there many times." And I said, "Yeah, you fought there twelve times. I remember every one of them. I was at all of them." Well, this got us into a conversation and we talked for a little while and finally he asked me, "How many pro fights have you had?"

"None."

"Well, then, how many amateur fights?"

"None."

He looked at me surprised. "And you're fighting Tino?"

I told him that Angelo had told me that Tino was a so-so fighter.

"So-So? His record is 19 and 0! He hasn't lost one yet!"

All of this had some time to work into my brain. Angelo had sent me out for my first fight against a local hero with an unblemished record whose abilities impressed none other than Willie Pep, one of the great fighters of all time. When they called me out, I went to my corner and looked out at the ring. There were blood splotches all over the canvas.

Tino and I went out to the center of the ring for instructions. The referee went through his litany of no rabbit punching or blows below the belt, all that stuff. Then he told us to go back to our corners and come out fighting at the sound of the bell. I went back to my corner and continued to steel myself. But Roth-Seiden, wasn't helping the cause. Right before the fight was to start, he came to my ear.

"Kid, you're really up against it here. The first time you get hit hard, just go down and stay there. It's no problem. We'll just start with a new name in Miami. Don't worry about it. No one will hate you for it." Here I was only seconds from my first fight and my manager was saying I'm in trouble and that I should take a dive for my own safety. It wasn't an arranged dive or anything. Roth-Seiden and I had hit it off for the first time on the drive to Tampa, and he just didn't want to see me get hurt. The last five seconds before the round began were chilling.

But when the bell sounded, I went out to center ring and began to fight. Fuertes was way stronger than me. Everything I tried, he would dip and counter-punch me. I'd throw a left and he would dip and whack me one in the body or throw a right over the top. I wasn't doing too well. All the while I was thinking of my manager's advice.

But his words could never jibe with the script I'd written for myself. I'd changed my name once and I wasn't going to go through

that again. Not that it had worked. When they announced me as
Danny Toriani, two guys from Buffalo looked up at me from ringside
and said, "Danny Toriani? You're Danny Diliberto! We've known
you since you were a kid." So a fall was just out of the question.

By the end of the first round, I had begun to figure Tino out. I
threw a couple of high jabs at the end of the round to test him. Sure
enough, every time I jabbed with the left, he would dip to my right
and throw a left hook to my body. At the very end of the round, I
threw a fake jab and then a right uppercut that he dipped right into.
I could feel his chin squash under the weight of the blow. Wham, he
went right to the canvas. He was out, but the bell saved him on the
count of eight.

In my corner, Roth-Seiden was now very excited. "Hit him in
the chin again. Hit him again!" When the bell rang for the second
round, I could see that Fuertes' eyes had not yet cleared. He hadn't
recovered from the blow. I knocked him down again, but he got up
on the eight count. By now I was real tired. I knew I had to finish him
off quick while I still could. I knocked him down two more times in
that round and that gave me the win by TKO. I only got paid $175
for the fight, but I was able to get down a 10-1 bet on myself for fifty
bucks so I made five hundred on that.

When Tino met canvas for the last time, the Tampa Armory went
wild. The local hero had gone down. I signed autographs all the way
to the dressing room. Once back there, Roth-Seiden made straight
for the pay phones and called Angelo. "Angelo, guess what happened here in Tampa?" And Dundee said, "what round did Danny
knock him out in?" The old fox knew what he was doing after all.

Back in Miami, I had gained respect in the gym. Some of these guys had refused to fight Fuertes and the idea that I had taken him out in two rounds earned me another look. But the victory had its downside. I could no longer get the easy preliminary fights that I needed to properly groom myself. I got a little frustrated with how things were and did some things I shouldn't have, like knocking out sparring partners in the gym. Angelo would come up to me and tell me, "Danny, you can't do this. You can't go around knocking people out in the gym. Some of these guys are your potential opponents."

My first fight in Miami was against Duane Simpson. He later became the U.S. Olympic boxing coach. I knocked him out, too. In our first fight, one of his stable mates, Billy Hall, showed up for the weigh-in because Duane couldn't get there on time. This made no sense, a stand-in fighter at the weigh-in, but it was okayed.

Billy went back and told Duane that he was fighting a skinny little kid with no chest. "You'll have an easy night," he told him. Duane came in over-confident and I knocked him out in the second round. My next fight was against Billy Hall. When Duane heard of the fight he went up to Billy and told him: "Now YOU'RE fighting a skinny little kid with no chest. Good luck!"

My first fight with Hall had come about under the same circumstances as my very first fight. Angelo Dundee had called me on a Tuesday morning and asked if I wanted to fight that night. "Billy Hall's opponent backed out. I need a fighter." So I agreed and the fight was on.

This was my third pro fight. Billy Hall had over thirty. This was a six-round fight and the first three rounds I pounded him. I hurt him, but he took it. He just refused to go down. Billy Hall was in great shape and he wouldn't wear down. This is when I discovered how little joy there is in being in the ring with someone who isn't tired, when you are exhausted. I had spent the entire previous night with my girlfriend Donna. She would go with me to do the roadwork, and then I would come back to the hotel and do my stomach exercises. My exercise routine finished every night with a workout on Donna. A lot of the old trainers wanted you to refrain from having sex for two weeks before a fight, but I never could go for that. It's just not natural. Besides, I was a hound. Once I overcame my natural shyness and discovered how marvelous women are, I wanted to be with them all the time. I fell in love with women and sex and they took up a lot of my time. As a result, when Dundee called, I wasn't ready for the later rounds.

When the bell rang for the fourth round my legs just said no. I forced myself up, but the last three rounds were pure survival. I won the first three, he won the last three, and we fought to a draw. This was the only one of my fourteen fights that I didn't win.

I fought Billy Hall three times. The second one was my revenge fight. After our draw I asked George when the next card was where I could get Billy and he told me two weeks. "I want him. I have to fight him again. Get me that fight." The two weeks went by and I trained really hard. This time I just beat him up. I stopped him in the third round and he was torn up. I cut his face and I hurt him. I had my revenge for the draw. I had three or four other fights, all uneventful wins, before I would face Hall again for the final time.

I knew he would be looking for blood, He didn't like that I had beaten him. No fighter ever likes seeing the referee raise the other guy's hand. On the Kid Gavalan - Tiger Jones card, I got to fight Hall again. This was at the Caralon Hotel on Miami Beach. This time, Hall came charging out of the ring after the first bell and I had to slip his hard right. I dipped and threw the right back at him but I caught him across the head and I could hear my hand snap again.

Angelo wanted to stop the fight after the first round, but I begged him to let me go on. He did and I managed enough points with my left to win the decision. That was the only fight where I needed a decision. The rest were knockouts or TKO's.

After the last fight with Hall, I had to wait months for the hand to heal. I spent my time at the track with George and with training my left hand. All the left was really good for was jabs and feints, though. My right was the powerhouse, accurate and hard. The broken bones were now taking their toll. My fist was no longer flush; it had knuckles that stuck out further than normal and that caused it to be even more fragile.

Fighting paid lousy unless you were the big name on the card, so I was still driving pizzas around at night. Dundee hated that, he said it put me out of shape and it made me look tired in the gym, so I had to quit. To pay the bills, I did some things with George Roth-Seiden. He was a bit of a hustler. He was a card player. He would have a group over to his house and they would sit around the swimming pool playing gin rummy.

I was introduced to the group as a member of the boxing stable and that I would be out there with them doing some sketching or painting. I would also be stealing looks at cards. I had a small rectangular eraser that I would use to send signals to George. If someone drew a card that could be used in a three of a kind I would hold the eraser the short way. If the card could be used in a run I would hold the eraser the long way. So George would know what cards his opponent needed by watching the draw pile and my eraser.

George's wife worked for Arthur Murray Dance Studios. She was one of the dancers on the weekly Arthur Murray television show. The Arthur Murray people had a poker game once a week into which George introduced me. George and I made sure we never sat next to one another.

The scam with this was that it was a friendly game, so after you folded your hand, no one cared if you looked at their cards. I would show my hand to anyone who had folded, so it was understood that you could show your cards to a folded player. George and I worked out a series of word signals that would allow us to broadcast hands to one another. "It's *just* not that way" meant a *jack*. "The *kind* of guy I want to be" was a *king*. And so on. This let us beat the game week after week and make a little extra money.

George also loved the horses. He was a decent handicapper, but he also had some moves there. He knew this rich guy who was in with us. This mark would come to the track with us and thought he was our partner. He would bet off of George. So George would go up and pretend to bet a horse that had absolutely no chance. He would come back from the window and tell us he had bet three hundred, one hundred for each of us, on this horse. The horse, of course, would lose and George would collect the hundred, he never bet, from the rich guy. He could make a hundred off this guy on several races a day. All he had to do was to pick a winner occasionally and actually make the bet.

This continued and even on days that he could not come to the track with us, our mark wanted to be in on our action. So we set it up so that whenever he didn't come with us, he was a winner. We'd go to him and say, "Hey, we won nine hundred today, here's your three hundred." We developed a pattern, where he lost when he came with us and won when he stayed home. These absentee wins kept his trust and inspired his presence with us at the track.

Meanwhile, my hand continued to hamper my fighting. I wound up breaking it four times in fourteen fights and finally Dundee sat me down for the speech. "Danny. You're a real good fighter, but you've just had some bad luck and the fighting is over. Your hands are just too fragile. You can do other things. If you continue to fight, your hands will only get worse. You're young, go make a life for yourself somewhere else." I took my stuff out of the gym and went back to my room and cried for the first time since I was a child.

Chapter Four
THE ARMY AIRBALL

I was still in Miami and still hanging around Dundee's gym. They wanted me to help groom young fighters, but I was too honest to be any good at that. I kept telling the ones with no talent that they should get into another line of work. This caused Dundee to have another talk with me. "Danny, not everyone is a Marciano. We need preliminary fighters as well as headliners. Stop scaring off the undercard!"

I needed some direction in my life, a new goal. I spent a lot of time trying to decide what to do with myself. Then Uncle Sam helped me with that decision by drafting me. In October of 1959, I got the "Greetings" letter. I had spent two years fighting for Dundee and now I would go fight for America.

When I got drafted, I went quietly. I was broke, but I refused to ask Angelo for any road money. I put a loaf of bread and a jar of peanut butter in a bag and I hit the highway to hitchhike back to Buffalo to report for duty. I got let off of one ride at around two in the morning in South Carolina. I stood there for a while with my thumb out and finally a car stopped and the guy asked me where I was going. When I told him he said, "No, sorry, I'm not going there." And he drove off towards the moon. It was late October, cold and drizzly, and I was miserable. I was standing out there getting wetter and colder by the moment.

About twenty minutes later that same car came back and pulled over. "I can go that way, after all," he said. "I just looked at the map and I can make that work, come on in." I was so tired, that I dozed off within minutes of getting in the car. The car was warm and dry and I was so relieved to be moving again that sleep came easily. His hand on my leg awakened me. It woke me in a start and I jerked and his hand moved, but I could see that he had driven us to a swamp somewhere and parked. We were nowhere near a highway and I didn't care for his plans.

"Get me out of here and take me back to a main road, NOW!" I demanded. He pleaded with me not to be mad, all that crazy stuff, but he could see I wasn't going to go along with him and he took me back to Highway 301. I got out and once again resumed the classic hitchhiker stance, leaning to one side with the thumb out and the bag slung over my back.

My hitchhiking continued on the two-lanes. This was before the interstate highway system had been built. It was also before folks got paranoid about picking up a stranger. Hitchhiking used to be a popular form of transportation and it was great. But then the country decided to fear strangers and this sea change in attitude ended a great era. Up until the mid-seventies, you could hitchhike almost as fast as you could drive somewhere. It was a whole lot faster than the bus and you got to meet some neat folks in the process. I never could put a finger on the circumstance that caused us to stop trusting one another to the point where a thumb out on the highway constituted a threat, but it happened real fast and the shoulders of the road became as lonely as midnight.

But in the fifties, it was still a valid and popular system, and I wound up going through the mountains of West Virginia with a local hot-rod who really knew the mountain roads. He knew how to accelerate in the curves to make the springs squat down and the car hug the road and he knew how to brake with the clutch to keep the rear end tight. He gave me more than a few frights, but he never seemed worried at all and he got me through the mountains as quickly as I imagine it can be done.

I finally got to Buffalo and the draft board. There I went through all the induction craziness, bending over naked with a room full of bent-over naked guys while an army doctor checked us out. Pronounced halfway fit due to ulcers, I was shipped off first to Fort Dix in New Jersey where they assigned me to Fort Hood in Texas for Basic Training. What a joke that was. A whole bunch of us from New York were all on the same bus and when we pulled into Ft. Hood, they lined us up outside the bus and Sergeant Bo Healer started pacing back and forth in front of us and growling. "All right, you fast talking wise guys from New York City, if any one or two of you think you're tough enough you can meet me on the lawn at dawn and nothing will ever be said about it. We can settle it real quick, I promise!"

So we all just stood there and wondered about this huge guy and soon we were assigned to our barracks and our beds and then we got another lecture, the same one, from our platoon sergeant. It's like they all had the same script. "All right you smart talking New Yorkers. I'm going to go in the john for five minutes and if any of you think you're tough, come see me in there and we can work it out. Nothing will ever be said."

Five minutes later he came out. "Okay, well I guess we got that straight." And he assigned one of us as an orderly. And *that* guy gets up and makes the same stupid speech! It was unbelievable. This boot camp looked like an idiot's convention where everyone only knew how to make a single threat. We knew that the deal here was to break down our individuality in order to glue us together as a team, a fighting force dependent upon one another, but this methodology seemed completely off-track.

It got worse, much worse. The Sergeants stayed drunk all the time and the men in the barracks would steal anything they could get their hands on. You couldn't turn your back or they would loot your stuff. Anyone with any authority abused it by issuing threat after threat. There was no respect for anyone as a man. You were treated like an animal.

After a few weeks of this crap, I just got up one day and sat on my footlocker and refused to move. I had decided to quit the Army. The Sergeant came up to me and said, "Diliberto! Get off your ass, get your gear on, and get out there with the men!"

"No."

"What do you mean, No?"

"No, I ain't going."

"What?"

"I quit."

"You can't quit, get out there."

"I quit, I ain't going out there. Do whatever you have to do, I don't care."

They let me sit there on my footlocker for two days. They figured I had flipped out. The orderly stayed clear of me, assuming I had gone mad and was possibly dangerous. After two days the Captain came in and stood before me. "Diliberto, I have to give you this order and tell you just how serious this is. If you disobey a direct order, you will face court martial on a charge punishable by five years in prison."

I thanked the Captain for his efforts. Bo Healer had tried to strangle me and convince me that way, but that hadn't worked. He had come storming up the stairs screaming that he was going to kill me, but I was ready for that madness. It fit the pattern. He did the same screaming as before about get off your ass and get out there and when I nodded no, he wrapped my jacket around my neck and picked me up. I just looked at him and finally he dropped me back to the footlocker and ordered me outside again.

Again I said, "No."

So Healer stormed out and I knew that the next visit would be from his boss, the Captain. After the Captain's visit a sergeant MP came and got me and put me in the stockade. The stockade had bunks all in a row, but not stacked on top of each other. At night it was real dark in there, and you had to go down some stairs and across a lit yard to get to the latrine. When I went to the latrine on the first night, I came back to find my bunk gone. It had been thrown out of the window into the slush. It was freezing rain that night and I had to go outside, get my bunk, and drag it back inside. My bed was all wet and cold and I had to lay there with the laughter all around me. These guys thought this was real funny.

I was pretty miserable. I figured my life was over when they court-martialed me and sentenced me to five years. I awaited transport to Leavenworth in the stockade while the Major took the time to review my case, as was required of every court-martial.

In the stockade, I played the hermit. I wanted nothing to do with anyone and I just stayed by myself. There was a nut case named McDaniels that harassed me all the time. He thought it was his personal job to screw me over. I'd be standing in line for chow and he would break in line in front of me, pushing me out of the way. Day after day this guy would mess with me. He even got a friend involved and they would both break in front of me in the chow line. The whole time, he was talking real bad to me; calling me everything vile on the planet and threatening to mess me up. The quieter I was with him, the worse it got.

So I got a case on about this guy. I hated him as much as I have ever hated anyone. I found out that at night I could lie on my back with my eyes looking at the ceiling and still see his bunk out of the extremities of my peripheral vision. I laid awake nights waiting on McDaniels to go to the bathroom. I was kept alert by the soap fights anyway. These guys would fling bars of soap at one another and they went whizzing above the bunks. I didn't want to get hit by one of the hard soaps, so I lay as flat as I could, face up.

Finally, after several days, McDaniels got up in the wee hours of the morning to go to the latrine. He went down the stairs, out of the darkness and into the light. This was the opportunity I had been looking forward to since I first encountered him. I followed his steps and waited in the darkness for his return.

I heard the latrine flush and he came out and crossed the lighted area towards me. I was invisible in the darkness. When he crossed out of the light, I was there and unleashed my right hand onto his chin. He was level when he hit the ground, out cold. I went back to my bunk and lay there grinning in the darkness. He never bothered me again.

After fifteen days, a Navajo sergeant picked me up and took me to headquarters to meet with the Major who had been reviewing my case. The Major said, "Diliberto, there are 181 men in your class of recruits and you have the highest marks of any of them. If it weren't for your ulcers, we would have already qualified you for Officer Training School. Out of all the guys who could have given me a case, I expected it least from you. What gives with this crap?"

"Well, sir, you have my records. You must know that there is something very wrong here." And he said, "Yeah, let's talk about it."

And I told him everything. I told him about the ridiculous bullies, the drunk Sergeants, the thieving recruits. I said, "How am I going to trust men in a foxhole that steal from me every chance they get? How can I trust my life to someone that steals my watch?" I told him about the guy whose rifle went off as he cleaned it and about the guy who couldn't toss the grenade over the wall and how he nearly killed us when it bounced across the top of the wall and only fell over at the last second before exploding. And I told him I just couldn't fit in with people like that.

The major said, "I can see you don't belong in the stockade." He called the Sergeant back into the room. "I want this man out right now. Put him in with another group and let's give this another go."

The Sergeant said he couldn't get me out until the next day and the Major went right down his throat with it. "I said NOW, Sergeant, and I mean it!" So the Sergeant took me and did some paperwork and put me in with another group. But it was the same stuff with a different set of faces. It was like these guys caught army disease as soon as they crossed into the fort.

This time, the bully was named Prevost. He picked on a fellow named Rizzo and led a group of guys who would beat up an effeminate recruit named Paul. They were brutal with him. I came back one night and Paul's nose was all bent and his face was bruised real badly. There was nothing he could do but take the beatings.

One day I saw Prevost steal Rizzo's wallet while Rizzo was in the can. Later that day I returned to the barracks as Rizzo was getting beat up by Prevost. I was tired of this guy, so I stood on the sidelines and yelled instructions to Rizzo as to what to do. Prevost soon took exception to this and turned to me with a scowl, "You want in on this, Diliberto?" And I said, "I thought you'd never ask." He dropped his guard on the first feint and I nailed him with a right hook to the chest on the second one. He went down hard, gasping for breath and unable to get any air. Soon he was crying. "Why'd you do that? Why don't you like me?" He sounded like a little girl.

I said, "I've been watching you, Prevost, You're nothing but a thief, a bully and a liar. There's nothing about you to like." After that I had it pretty good. The orderly was afraid of me so he wouldn't issue me any chores. While the rest of the group swabbed floors, I would nap in my bunk.

But I was again resigned to quitting this army. I was just totally incompatible with the lifestyle that it fostered. I had never been one to back off from a good scam, but scams require planning and intelligence and style to carry off. These guys were just a bunch of lazy crooks and degenerates. So I went on sick leave every day. Finally, the brass called me in for a talk. "Diliberto, you're suspected of malingering. If you go on sick call tomorrow, you're going back to do your five years."

I said, "Well, I feel fine right now, but if I feel bad in the morning, I'm going on sick call." The next morning I went on sick call. So the Sergeants started playing these games. One would come up to me: "You don't have to do this anymore. They're going to discharge you." But another one would tell me I had to buckle down or they weren't going to let me out, ever. I kept a deadpan face every time.

After a few more days of this, one of the Sergeants came up to me. "Get your stuff together, you're being discharged." Someone knew what the story was, because they gave me an honorable discharge. I even got full veteran benefits.

Chapter Five
ACTION AND OVENWARE

Mike DiJohn was one of the friends I made during the boxing days. Mike was a great fighter and at one time a true threat as a really big heavyweight. He looked mean, but that was just his huge body talking. He was actually one of the gentlest men I had ever known, and always avoided trouble because he was so concerned that he might hurt somebody real bad.

I pulled into a gas station in Miami one day and found Mike there pumping gas. Boxing paid really lousy unless you were on television and he had to pump gas, this great big fighter, to make ends meet. Around that time, the movie *The Hustler* had made things on the road pretty mean. Folks who had spent years reliably losing to road players suddenly decided that they should get tough, like in the movie. So I asked Mike what he was making pumping the gas. When he said, "One-fifty a week," I told him, "I'll give you two-fifty just to hang around with me!"

So from then on he traveled with me and sat by the table and watched me play. When folks realized we were together, it completely prevented any trouble. Nobody wanted a piece of this guy. We went to probably five hundred bars between Miami and Key West and only suffered trouble once.

What happened there was that I beat this place in Key Largo, and when we went outside to leave, there were two guys there and they put the gun on us. One of the thugs had a gun pointed at Mike's heart and the other guy started kicking him with everything he could muster. Well, Mike just reacted to the kicks and knocked the guy out cold with a single swat. Then the guy with the gun started yelling that he was going to kill us.

Mike felt like his options were pretty limited. The thug said he was going to shoot no matter what, to revenge the knockout, so Mike figured he might as well act. Better to go down in a charge than in a cower. So he charged the guy with the gun and the guy, seeing this very mean-looking mountain coming for him, panicked and pulled the trigger and shot Mike in the thigh. The bullet went right through, leaving holes on both the front and back of the leg, and Mike started running around, with blood gushing profusely out of his leg, screaming that he had been shot. Meanwhile, the gunman was scared silly because now he had gone and shot somebody, so he ran off into the night and I drove Mike to the hospital.

When he came to after the surgery I was in his room, sitting at his bedside. He opened his eyes and looked up at me and before he could speak I said, "Mike, you better go back to pumping gas." He nodded his head and went to sleep again. I slipped five hundred in his coat and drove away to never hear from him again. In this lifestyle, you lose friends to inertia. People can't look you up when you're moving all the time.

Around this time, there was a player in Pittsburgh named Bernie Schwartz. Bernie was a huge guy with a hawk's nose and his poolroom there in Pittsburgh was known as 'The Hawk's Nest." He threw a big Nine Ball tournament there and every night after the tournament was over and he closed the room, the real action would start—the gambling between players.

Bernie was always one of the players in action and he was very tough action. He had beaten Irving Crane twice in the U.S. Masters that year and he was playing superb Nine Ball as well. That year, every road player that came into the Hawk's Nest got sent home broke.

We thought that his luck might change, because he wasn't just playing any old road scofflaw that rolled in the door. He was playing the acknowledged best players in the country! But he wasn't losing! He picked out a new victim every night and plucked them solid bald. In fact, he took on Ronnie Allen for five straight nights.

This was a problem for Ronnie. The guys he had talked into staking him against this local nobody named Bernie Schwartz, were mob guys who really detested seeing their money go away night after night. They lost four or five sets a night at four to five hundred dollars per set for five straight nights! Ronnie was sweating blood.

On the sixth night of this marathon, Ronnie finally won his first match against Bernie. The wise guys were cracking a grin, Ronnie started to feel loose and he knew he could do something with this Bernie character. Bernie looked over at him, unscrewed his stick, and said he was tired and quit the game.

One of the mob guys, this big gorilla like you see in the movies, calmly rose from his seat and walked over and pulled a fire extinguisher off the wall. He threw it across three aisles and it landed in the middle of a table and ruptured, spattering white foam everywhere. Then he kicked the coke machine and it looked like the machine was hit by a bazooka. There was nothing Bernie and his wife could do but sit there and watch this guy go around their room and take it apart.

Glasses and bottles went off like firecrackers and stools flew everywhere. By the time the big wop got to the door and left, the room looked like Delta Force had been there to rescue a hostage. Everything was broken. Bernie put the room back together as best he could and the tournament continued the next day, but without Ronnie.

I ran into Ronnie Allen again the following May in Long Beach. I had gone out there for a Nine Ball tournament that didn't pay well and the action was absent; so nobody made out and there was a lot of grumbling. The only good thing that happened the entire week was when Joe, a player from Philadelphia, approached me with some business. He had a backer he wanted to dump and he wanted me to be the catalyst for the action. "If I ask you to play some One Pocket after the tournament, it's business. I'm dumping my guy."

At midnight, he came up and asked me to play and the game was on. But the problem we had was that there are two strokes in pool that are tough to beat. One is the 'give up' stroke, and the other is the dump stroke. Joe, attempting to dump, couldn't miss anything. At 4 AM we were dead even. Finally he came over and whispered to me that I just didn't play well enough and we would have to quit.

I looked at him and said, "No, we don't. Just quit the dump and play me on the square." He did, and I beat him out of four hundred bucks in an hour, and needless to say, he wasn't in on the cash. But the rest of the tournament was a waste of time. Worse, after it was over, there wasn't another tournament for weeks, so we all needed to find a spot where there was enough gambling to tide us over.

Ronnie came over to a group of us exploring options and said that they were gambling big in Mobile, so everyone tossed that idea around for a minute and soon the crowd was ready to hit the road to Alabama. But then, Richie Florence mentioned another spot and we all considered that one for a while and then Eddie Burton came over and said he had just talked to Jimmy Mataya and he had told him the action was sky high in Detroit. This got our attention, because if Mataya said there was great action, then you could believe it, because it took a lot to get Jimmy excited. He could lose ten grand and be no more upset than someone who just ran out of toothpaste. Mataya would shoot his last barrel at you and then just keep on going.

In a few days, the entire California contingent was in the *Rack and Cue* in Detroit. This room, home for years to guys like Cornbread Red, was actually two rooms, a poolroom and a card room, separated by a door. We discovered that Mataya hadn't exaggerated a bit. There were some real wealthy guys in the card room and some of that money wafted out into the poolroom whenever one of the card men wandered out there to be entertained by the goings-on of the stick-toting outlaws.

The day I arrived, Jimmy Mataya was playing Jew Paul on a big old snooker table with bleachers full of sweaters on both sides. They were playing Six Ball for sky-high money. Jimmy and Jew Paul actually had to stand around between games and wait until everyone settled their bets before they could go on to the next rack because there was so much complex side action going on in the bleachers. After the bets were settled, time still had to be allotted for new bets to be made, so there was a lot of standing around going on between racks.

The scene was surreal. There were guys in the stands with paper bags full of cash. One guy even had a hard-shell suitcase crammed with dough. After every game, he opened that suitcase for either a deposit or a withdrawal. The action went on for weeks. It was heavenly.

Then one day, we were all minding our own business trading cash around and the law came in and closed the place up. Here we were a thousand miles from home and we've got no action. On the road, you need action almost every day or the nut will eat you up. Motel rooms, gas, food, cleaners—all that stuff mounts up real quick when you're living out of a suitcase.

Well, the owner of the poolroom came out and said: "Boys, stick around. They didn't do this right. I'll get an injunction and be open tomorrow." Ronnie Allen didn't believe him and took off for Mobile with a few of his friends. The rest of us stayed in Detroit and sure enough, in about three days, the guy reopened the room and we were back in action.

I got a game with Jew Paul. When it was over I had won $22,000 in a game called *One Ball in the Side*. It's played like Straight Pool, but the one has to go in the side. In those days in Detroit my twenty-two grand really wasn't much of a score. But

ACTION AND OVENWARE

Jew Paul had had enough so he quit me. He said, "I'm not going to play you anymore. But you're going to stick around here, you're going to bet on my games, and you're going to go broke. When you do—come and talk to me."

So I laughed at that and cut up the money with my partners. But sure enough, I bet on a match Paul was in and lost all my money. Eddie Burton had gotten in a match with Paul and told me he was stealing. I bet on Eddie and lost the whole wad. I was broke. So I went up to Paul and told him his prediction was good and I was broke. Paul took me to the coffee shop across the street and laid out his plan over a steak dinner. He said, "I'm giving you four hundred dollars now. I want you to go to Boston tomorrow and meet Bernie Schwartz there."

"Bernie's in Boston? Why?" and Paul told me he was there selling ovenware. "Ovenware? Bernie Schwartz? Why? He had a super year last year—must have won at least thirty grand."

Jew Paul put his coffee down and delivered his punch line. "Now he makes that in a week. Just do me a favor. Go to Boston, get with Bernie and call me in a few days and tell me what you think." Jew Paul was a real nice guy, but he covered his ass. He gave me some traveling money along with the airfare. When he took me to the airport the next day he convinced me to 'let him use' my Balabushka cue while I was in Boston. This gave him some collateral for his money and assured him that he would see me again.

Schwartz picked me up at the airport and on the way to the Holiday Inn in Framingham he explained the whole scheme. Every day was the same. Up at 6 AM, breakfast with a crew of salesmen, and then into the businesses with ready cash. Once there, you could sell both to the business and to the employees. Before the day began, we would drop by the warehouse to load our cars with ovenware sets.

Now this wasn't bad ovenware at all. It looked real good and all of the salesmen had these gorgeous printed brochures and all, so it looked real legit. And it was a good deal. We were selling a 49-piece ovenware set for $15.00 off of a brochure that quoted the price as a bargain at $89.95! The pitch was that the sets were left over from a local home-ware show so it was cheaper to sell them at a loss than it was to ship them back. It was a real moneymaker. The plan worked like a pyramid plan with the crew leader getting a share of what his guys sold and the recruiters getting a share of the crew leaders take and so on. It was *Nine Ball Amway*.

After a few months of this I called Jew Paul. "Paul, I gotta have my own crew." I had lots of friends and relatives around the country that weren't doing all that well and I figured I could get a crew together and it would work out for all involved.

When I got my own crew, we went to work Indianapolis. I'd take the crew out for breakfast, following the formula Bernie taught me, and then drop them off in promising areas. After the day's work, everyone came in at five and we would all count up the money and go get a good meal. My guys were doing real well and we had to reload the ovenware stocks every day.

Meanwhile, a couple of guys on the road weren't doing too well. They were traveling together and their luck turned so sour that they couldn't buy a roll in a bakery. Jew Paul turned them on to me and they called up and I said, "Yeah, come on over." I figured at least they could earn some money to get a road stake going. So they showed up in Indianapolis and it was like old home week except we were bored. One night one of the guys wondered out loud how we could get some hookers.

Well, I knew a guy in town that could get anything as long as it was illegal, so we called him up and ordered four girls to be sent to the room. While we were waiting for them to show, we started wondering about how we would decide which guy gets to pick which girl when they get to the room. So we drew straws and I got the shortest one. When the girls showed up, mine was so ugly that my dick went to hide somewhere out back 'til she left. I just sat and talked to her. She was like the girl your momma wanted you to date in high school, the one with the *great personality*.

From Indianapolis, I traveled west again to Bakersfield, California. My whole crew followed me out there and I rented nice rooms for everyone at the Holiday Inn, as that was the whole secret to that racket, to look real respectable, and have a nice motel name and phone number on your card. Then it doesn't seem at all to be a scam, but looks and feels legit.

The only problem with the hotel in Bakersfield was that the Thursday night fights didn't get cabled into your room. The fights were taking place in L.A., only 130 miles away, but to see them you had to leave the room and go down to the bar where they played on a big TV on the wall.

ROAD PLAYER

I was sitting there one Thursday night and some guys were betting on the red corner, or the blue corner, or whatever, and one of them asked me if I wanted to bet with them. So I figured what the hell, and started betting just by chance on the red or blue corner. I knew nothing about the fighters, there was no sheet or anything; so it was just picking a corner and laying your money down.

I lost every bet and two guys there pinned me as a sucker. They saw we were having a good time and I was losing every bet and still buying the drinks. So after the fights were over, one of these guys looked at me and said, "Hey, if you want to get even there's a bowling alley down the street." I hadn't bowled for over ten years, so I said, "Well, I tell you what, if there's also a pool room nearby, I'll bowl you the same amount that we play pool for."

He said, "Yeah, I play pool, too, and there's tables in the bowling alley." The only thing left to do was to set the stakes, so I asked him what he wanted to do. He said he didn't care so I said, "Okay, let's bowl for four hundred and then play pool for four hundred."

He didn't have that much cash on him, but he couldn't let a sucker slide, so he got Sonny, the bartender at the Holiday Inn, to stake his action. We went off to gamble and on the way over there, everything was just fine. These guys were laughing and joking around with me like we had been friends for life. Then we got to the lanes.

The guy I was to bowl went downstairs and came back up with a bag, a ball, and shoes. At the time, that was a big thing in bowling, to have your own gear. It was the equivalent of walking into a poolroom with a leather case under your arm. He sat down and polished his Black Beauty while I went around and picked out a house ball.

74

We flipped a coin to see whether we would bowl or play pool first and he won the flip and picked bowling. I went out there and got lucky and my first seven balls were strikes. Now this guy was a pretty good bowler, but he wasn't keeping up with my strikes and after my first three strikes, his buddies stopped with the jokes and the laughing and things began to firm up between us.

They all began to realize that their sucker wasn't a sucker and they started to get a little bit nasty. I kept telling them that I hadn't bowled in ten years, but that I've always been a pretty good athlete and they began to think this was bullshit. In the back of my mind, I knew that we hadn't even played the pool yet, that we're still on his game and already they're getting testy.

I bowled a 257 and he bowled a 218, which is pretty darn good, but I won and we had to go play Nine Ball. I was trying to be a nice guy about it all, but he had no hope on the pool table. I robbed him easily. The problem was that I then had to get in the car with these guys to ride back to the Holiday Inn bar and tell the bartender that he had lost his money.

These guys were nasty as hell all the way back. They weren't happy at all. We went into the bar and Sonny the barkeep smiled up at us and said, "Hey, guys, how'd it go?"

One of them looked at me and barked: "Sonny, this son-of-a-bitch is a no-good Yankee hustler and you ain't paying him."

And Sonny goes, "Hey, if I lost, I'm paying him."

And the mad guy said, "If you even think about paying him, I'm gonna bust your head and that's what I ought to do to this stinking Yankee hustler."

Which is when I got involved. "Whoa, buddy, hold it. A couple of hours ago you thought you could beat me bowling and playing pool and now you want to get physical. How do you know you can win at that?"

He said, "Come outside and I'll show ya!"

We went outside and he charged me, so I sidestepped him and hit him with a right square on the chin. He dropped to the parking lot like a sack of potatoes. When he got up a few minutes later he was all groggy and shaking his head from side to side and he came over to me and said, "Well, I had that coming. I deserved it." We went back into the bar and told Sonny to pay me. I went to my room with my eight hundred and slept. Morning was only a few hours away.

The next day I walked into a music shop and hit the owner with the full spiel about the ovenware, how we had just had a show in town and couldn't afford to ship it back, the whole nine yards. While I was hitting the owner with this a guy walked in and says, "Hey, where's Junior?" And the guy I was talking to said, "Where do you think he is; he's in the poolroom as always!"

The interruption left and we continued with our business and the guy was interested in the ovenware. He wanted to get a bunch of it, and then Junior walked in with a cue case. So I said, "I tell ya what. I had my eye on this clarinet and that banjo over there. I don't know Junior, here, how well he plays or anything, but I'll play him equal amounts of money for my ovenware sets against the clarinet and banjo. We can play Straight Pool to a hundred points. If he wins, you get the ovenware and if I win I get the instruments."

ACTION AND OVENWARE

They jumped all over that and daddy closed up the music shop and we all walked down the street to the poolroom. The kid broke the rack and I ran 78 right off the bat and won the game easily. The owner thought this was all kind of cute, having Junior put in his place and shown his rank in the pecking order of pool, so there were no problems and I became the proud owner of a clarinet and a banjo.

The next morning, I realized that after two boring months of selling ovenware, two nice things had happened to me in poolrooms in two days! I called up Jew Paul: "Paul, send me my cue stick. I've had it with the ovenware. I'll give Bernie the money I owe ya." I went back on the road again.

This ovenware gig was a doomed effort from the start. I never liked the nine to five and this was for sure nine to five and then some. In fact, I hated regular jobs so much that they gave me a rash. God's truth. When I was nineteen I was working a construction gig and I got a rash on the back of my leg and it got so bad I had to go to the Doctor about it. He looked at it and we talked a little and he told me it was psychosomatic. I got this rash because working makes me tense and nervous. In other words, I don't like it. The doctor says to cure the rash; I have to quit working the job. Since I believe in doing what the doctor tells me, I quit the job and have generally avoided nine to five all my life.

Chapter Six
DISCIPLINES AND GUIDELINES

Johnston City only lasted a month every fall, so we all needed something to do the rest of the year. For most of us, that meant traveling the road. Johnston City provided the stops, the knowledge of how to create and sustain the action, and the contacts that allowed all sorts of action to be created throughout the country.

There was much to be learned before committing oneself to the blacktop. Even this loose of a lifestyle had limits; constraints within which one must be contained. Some of these 'rules' were more obvious than others. One of the basics is to never play a man in front of his wife. She'll always bring him up short and you won't win as much as you should. Wait until the guy is in charge of his own wallet before mounting an assault on it. Wives can be like the gatekeepers to hell when they start seeing the grocery money being tossed across the table. The one exception I ever saw to this rule was Ted Elias. His wife controlled their bankroll and when Ted was losing, she would get on his case and tell him to quit dogging it and make him keep playing, chasing the dough.

Never play someone who doesn't think they can win. They have to be good enough to think they can come back, or they'll quit the game before you can win enough for dinner. The best marks are skilled players who have enough larceny in their hearts to rob you.

Don't be fooled into thinking that hustling is like you've seen it in the movies. That kind of stalling is too time-consuming and can backfire quickly. It is far easier to just stroll into a strange room and declare yourself the toughest player on earth. Demand to play the best that they've got and tell them up front that you're going to whip their ass. Ronnie Wiseman of today's generation has it down right. He walks up to the barman, tosses him a quarter and says, "I'm here to gamble at pool for money. Call someone." There's no need to sneak around when the pool ego will always rise to a challenge. All you have to do is to become that challenge.

Because you'll be playing the best player around, you have to stick to a betting formula that will allow you to maximize your winnings. This formula demands that you play the local hero, but play him cheap. That's because the real action is on the rail. You don't just bet the mark, you bet all of his friends and relatives and all the folks who think he can't be beaten. Your major income comes from the sweaters. The fellow holding the cue is just a means to an end. So you want to play him cheap, because if all he's got is a hundred dollars and you play him twenty a game, you can knock yourself out of action in only five games. That's what you call unrealized potential and you must avoid that. You need to maximize each visit to a new room and stay until you vacuum every bankroll in the place.

You never want to leave after firing only a few barrels. So play the guy for five bucks a game. Then instead of firing five times at the rail you get to shoot in that direction twenty times. This is the kind of rule that can make the difference between remaining free on the road and sacrificing yourself to the nine to five.

If you are going into a room where the action could turn violent, you do two things. First, always play with a cue you can sacrifice.

Second, check the size of the bathroom window. This way if you start to get nervous about the situation you can tell someone to watch your cue while you go to the bathroom, shimmy out the window and drive away alive. They get your cheap cue and you get the cash and your head. I used the rear exit in Kentucky and told the story to a friend who went through the same spot some months later and tried to do the same thing. When he went to the bathroom they had installed bars on the window, so he was trapped. He was playing on air and barely got out of there alive.

Johnston City was a classroom for roadmen. Most who came were not tournament players. Fatty used to deride the tournament players as guys with no heart. He called them hot dog players. He always claimed that Mosconi was a lightweight who only played pool for fun. There was no big money to be had in tournaments for most of us, so life on the road was the only available option for players without sponsors. These men spent their entire lives devoted to a sport that had been huge in the twenties and thirties and then died. It once again blossomed, only briefly, after Paul Newman endeared the Fast Eddie persona, but it hasn't threatened anyone with tournament wealth in three-quarters of a century. Pool has been a promise that is almost kept, an image that never quite gains focus. No one ever galvanized the industry into supporting the level of pro competition that would make the marketplace sizzle, so the only thing tournaments got you, was queered action on the road if someone recognized your face from a magazine or television.

DISCIPLINES AND GUIDELINES

There are a lot of rules that road partners live by. Often, one of these is that partners are not 'in' on losses, only wins. This means you must play well and hold up your end of the deal, because you have to share your wins with your partner, but you have to eat all of your own losses. If you make a bad game, you must swallow it alone and that makes you a better game maker. This is a great discipline to develop, and truly required when you're on the road with someone who may not respect the affection that you have for your cash.

If someone turns you on to a spot and tells you whom to play and gives you the details on how to make the game, then you pay that person a *jellyroll,* a percentage of whatever you win in that spot. That percentage is not fixed. You pay more for an easy match than for a tough one. If a guy sends you in somewhere that he says you are 'stealing,' then he expects a bigger payoff.

There is a basic law about checks and it goes like this: if a guy runs out of money and wants to play on a check, don't do it if the game is tough and you could lose. You never risk winning an airball against losing your cash. But if you are stealing from the guy—if he's a sucker—go ahead and take the check. You aren't risking your cash and the check *could* be good.

Always watch out for larceny. This is particularly crucial if you decide to back someone else with your money. Lots of guys find it easier to win by losing. Dump artists were everywhere in the old days. A backer could have a good run going with a guy and suddenly be broke when his man turned against him. A lot of backers turned sour because of this stuff and refused to back even great players, if those players had the reputation of being turncoats.

ROAD PLAYER

Ronnie Allen earned that reputation. I backed Ronnie in a losing effort against a fellow that he wanted to play one-handed and give away the seven-ball as well. Ronnie tried this bet all night and wound up losing all my cash. Some years later, he was trying to talk another backer into the same proposition against the same player. He asked me for support during this argument and all I could do was remind him that he had gone broke once before on this same bet. "Oh, Danny!" he cried: "I was *dumping* that time!"

Once in Johnston City, Ronnie was flown in by a guy who had his own airplane. This fellow really liked to bet big. He knew Ronnie could create the action, so he flew him in and within four days of staking Ronnie against all comers, this guy had been relieved of about $40,000 worth of wallet pressure. On the fifth day of this beating, he went up to Ronnie and said, "Ronnie, you dumped me. To lose like that you had to dump me." And Ronnie looked him square in the eye and said, "You know what your problem is? You don't know that dumping and dogging it look the same."

One of the rules that I formed early on, was to never do anything that could get me killed or put in jail. This rule was developed after a little incident in Canada. I had a friend in Buffalo, named Paul, who had called me to see if I could get any action at Blue Bonnet Raceway in Montreal. Blue Bonnet itself was just too small a track to hold much action. Our bets there would have killed the odds. I knew some bookies in Buffalo that I could get down with on most stuff, so I called them and told them I was going fishing in Canada

82

and wanted to play the ponies at night for a little recreation and asked if they would take the bets long-distance. I knew they wouldn't take too long to decide this. All bookies love horse action. The odds are much better for them there than in a head to head contest like football where it's a coin-flip at worst for the bettors. With eight or so horses on the track for any one race, the odds are sleeping heavily in the bookie's bed. Plus, it's easy action to lay off if the bets become too one-sided.

The bookies were in and the trip was on. Paulie had a pocket full of jockeys at this track who were willing to do some work with us. They had been holding horses back for a while and now were going to let them loose for us in exchange for getting a forty dollar win bet in their names on each race. Paulie and I checked into a nice Holiday Inn in Montreal and every night at the track we were scoring big. After all, we were bookie fishing with the hook already in the mouth. We spent our days around the pool deciding what races to bet and setting up the jockeys for the night's action.

There might be a jockey on a good horse in the race we were betting, who wasn't in on the heist. If he ran well, he could ruin our bets, so the jockeys on our team would block these guys out, run into them; do whatever was required to make sure that they didn't piss in the beer. We absolutely had the nuts on this whole deal. The guys controlling the horses were working for us, so we held the keys to the vault. We were making away with around four thousand a day and were just getting started when the bottom dropped out.

Around the fifth day, I spent the morning doing a little shopping, picking up some nice shoes, a suit or two, and ordering some tailored shirts. On the drive back to the hotel I was feeling pretty good about life in general. Then, when I got out of the car, little Al, one of the jockeys who were controlling our horses, met me in the parking lot. I figured he had some information for me about the races, but he surprised me. He said, "What's going on with you and Paul? The cops have him in your room."

I should have taken off, but I couldn't think of any reason the cops would have a beef with us. Our bookies were in the States, so there was no one to cause us trouble in Canada. There was no way this was about the track business, so I went to the room to check things out and the cops grabbed me, too. Paulie and I were hand-cuffed and sat down in the corner of the room. The hotel manager was screaming in French, everyone was looking real concerned, and I didn't even know who called this meeting or why we were there.

It turns out that Paulie had been stealing towels from a maid's cart and she had noticed it and, sure enough, he had a suitcase full of towels that the cops had opened up on the bed and were staring into like it was full of the crown jewels. Here we were copping thou-sands at the track with crooked jockeys and the freaking cops were busting us for stealing towels! Paulie had crammed forty-five of these cheap towels into a suitcase. The cops hauled us off to jail on Friday night and our arraignment wasn't scheduled until Monday, so we would lose three nights worth of action for about a twelve grand hit over the weekend alone.

I was sitting in this little cell with a steel cot and a bare light bulb that never went out, thinking about how much those towels cost us. On Monday, they put us in a paddy wagon with a bunch of guys accused of all sorts of malevolence and we went to court. Surely, I thought, the judge will see the silliness of incarcerating a towel thief, then slap our wrists and make us pay for the towels before releasing us back to the track.

Instead, he set a trial date for fourteen days later and sent us to Bordeaux prison where they held us awaiting trial in a dungeon full of Canada's castoffs. I was in a cell with a solid iron door that only had one little slit in it and no windows. It was a very dark and depressing place. The only break we got was when they let out into the yard for four hours a day, time which I spent reminding Paulie that if it weren't for his klepto-towel act we would be in the hot tub at the hotel probably accompanied by women and wine. In the yard, you could interact with other prisoners, and we found this one guy who had been there for eighteen months for stealing a single pair of pants from a store. This was when we really started to sweat it.

It turns out that French-Canadian law is real strict and tough. Back then, they had the death penalty and two guys were gassed at the prison while we were there. The consensus among the prisoners was that we would probably get five years for the towels. *Five years!* I went to Paulie. "Don't worry, Paulie. You won't do any time. If they give us five years, you are dead at my hand!" I just couldn't believe it, but we were assured by then that the prisoners knew their stuff about the law and prison time.

Finally our trial date arrived and we went before the judge. His name was Sorrentino and seeing that name was like a shaft of light from heaven. I was feeling real good about that, the Italian name, until one of the other prisoners said: "Shit, this is Sorrentino, the

Hanging Judge." My outlook headed due south. This whole ridiculous ordeal was looking as bad as it possibly could. The way things were going for us, it actually seemed probable that we were going to hell for five years for pinching terry cloth. Naturally, the worst that could happen did. After the arguments were over, we stood silent before Judge Sorrentino and he looked down on us and found us guilty. Then he sentenced us to five years in prison.

My world went dark. I absolutely could not comprehend the situation. I kept thinking: 'All this because I had a roommate who is so crooked that he couldn't resist the opportunity to steal a few towels,' and now a French ape had me by the shackled arm and was leading me out of the court to do five years in that dark little cell! My head was spinning and my legs felt numb and thick. As we started through the little gate that leads away from the main court area the Judge quietly asked, "How long would it take you to get out of Montreal?" The ape came to a halt and we turned around to face the judge. "Your honor?" I stammered. I couldn't believe what I had heard. Was there going to be a chance here? And he asked again, "How long will it take you to get out of Montreal? If I suspend the sentence can you be gone by midnight and never return to Montreal?"

"Your Honor, if you'll remove these chains and open that door, I'll start running right now and I won't stop until I'm out of Canada." Paulie and I were out of town long before dark. We hopped a bus to Buffalo and I never spoke to him again. We had won $36,000 in just the few days that we were in action, but we left many times that amount on the table. One of these days I'm going to go throw towels on Paulie's grave.

Chapter Seven
PLAYING IT STRAIGHT FOR A WHILE

I married my first wife, Francine, in 1962 and stayed faithful to her for five years. My son Danny was born on December 11, 1963, the anniversary of my first fight. Soon Francine, Danny and I moved from Buffalo to Miami. I preceded them to Miami and bluffed my way into a job as a draftsman in a steel rule and die place. I studied some books and learned enough to get the job.

I sent for the family and stayed with the job for a while, until I could relearn the Miami scene and start making enough money playing pool to quit. There was enough local action then that I did all right, at least better than the forty hours a week of drafting. Every fall I went to Johnston City and the bars in Miami would call me whenever a player came in looking for some action. I cleaned out a lot of road players and sent them home with the money for a bus ticket. Plus, I was running a poolroom. Ted Johnson and his wife Ellie ran the Family Billiard Center and they relied on me. I had asked them for a job and they gave me one as the manager.

I stayed loyal to Francine until one night I got a call from the Boots and Saddle. They said they had a player there that had beaten the locals and wanted a piece of me. I went over and there were two guys waiting for me and there was a really pretty girl with them.

They were from West Virginia. We made a wager on some sets of Nine Ball and I beat them. The whole time we were playing the girl was giving me the eye. The next day I couldn't get her out of my mind. I was at the Family Billiard Center the next night and I couldn't think of anything but her. So, on a lark, after we closed I went back to the Boots and Saddle hoping to find her there.

When I walked in the three of them were there. The girl was sitting at one end of the counter and the two guys were beside her. When the guys saw me come in they held up their hands. "No thanks, Danny, we've had all of you we can handle." And I told them, "No, this isn't about that." And I sat down next to the girl and started chatting her up.

"What's the deal with these guys you're with?"

"They're just friends."

"Well, tell them you're leaving."

When we got in my car she asked me what was on my mind. "Well, I thought we might get something to eat, then grab a bottle of wine and get a room somewhere. I want you tonight."

That was fine with her and that was the first time I cheated on Francine. After that, it seemed there were girls everywhere I went, waiting to get naked with me. It just became part of the action. Find a poolroom, get some action, find a girl, and get some more action. It went on like that for five or six years.

Running the Family Billiard Center was something I found easy to do. It was natural to fall into the rhythm of running the room. But it was still a nine-to-five sort of deal, so eventually I had to resign the job and go back on the road full-time. I split from Francine in 1970 and went traveling with Gary Penkowski. But I maintained contact with the family and sometimes I had Danny flown to where I was.

PLAYING IT STRAIGHT FOR A WHILE

In the 60's and early 70's California was a hot state for pool. There were a lot of good players out there and they would create action and generate enough interest to drive tournaments. Richie Florence had been telling me for a couple of years that California was heating up and some of the action in Southern California could rival what had been the hot spots of the earlier generation like Philadelphia, Chicago, or Norfolk.

I made my first trip out there in April of 1966. Burbank looked like paradise. The weather was perfect. Two guys had teamed up to throw a sixteen player round-robin Straight Pool invitational. They paid all of the player's expenses for the trip and put us up, two to a room, in a Travel Lodge. They wanted to treat everyone properly, so they guaranteed every player a minimum of $800 prize money. My roommate for the event was Richie Florence and it was good that Richie and I were compatible. This was another long event, twenty-eight days, and if your roommate was a pain in the ass it could be like doing time.

The tournament was held in a building that looked like an old warehouse. They fixed it up inside and put in bleachers and even had a room set up with practice tables. This tournament gained a bit of notoriety, not just because the promoters brought Willie Mosconi out of retirement to play, but because of the deal that Willie cut for himself to show up. He would get $10,000 as an appearance fee plus 5% of the nightly gate and whatever prize monies he might win. The tournament was an important one and paid a handsome five thousand dollars for first, but Mosconi's deal meant that he would out-earn the winner even if he never pocketed a ball.

That's how big a draw the Mosconi name had become. Having Mosconi there brought out the stars to watch us play. Fred Astaire was often there. He was a friend of Mosconi's and loved pool and played well himself, so it was no surprise to see him in the audience night after night. Lots of the local heavies showed up. It wasn't unusual to be chalking up under the eyes of James Caan, Burt Lancaster, Richard Conte, or even Judy Garland. One night Richie was talking about Astaire, about how the guy danced so marvelously. I said I wished that I had that much talent. This caused a big grin to wash across Florence's face. "You want to dance like Astaire?" "No," I said, "I want to play pool as well as he dances."

The tournament had two promoters. A money guy named Arnie Risen and a Tournament Director named Arnie Satin. Risen arranged the sponsors and the venue and all the business stuff while Satin ran the day-to-day of the tournament. Satin was originally from New York City and Mosconi, from Philadelphia, took an immediate dislike to him that intensified every time they had contact.

Once Mosconi got on your case about something, it would never die. He would start in on you and was just bulldog-tenacious about lecturing you on his disapproval of your shortcomings. He was like a bad parent who would never let the slightest trespass drop. He would drill on the same criticism for days after the malfeasance occurred that gave birth to his tirade. Satin had dared a transgression early on; with a call on a hit that Mosconi claimed was so wrong, he should be arrested.

From there on, Satin could find no favor with Willie. After the first week, Mosconi announced that Satin would no longer be al-

PLAYING IT STRAIGHT FOR A WHILE

lowed to referee any match that Willie was playing. Mosconi asserted that Satin had greasy hands and he wasn't going to play Straight Pool with balls that had grease spots on them. It really bugged Satin that Mosconi would act this way, especially after he had agreed to such a handsome financial package to bring Mosconi out for the event. And it kept getting worse every day. Mosconi ignored the tournament rules and played whatever way he wished. There was a rule against multiple tic safeties, but when the referee called a foul on it, Mosconi howled that *those* weren't *his rules*.

Satin was as busy as he could be. This was a big tournament and he and Risen did everything from selling tickets to scoring and refereeing. After the first few days, Satin became obviously worn from the stress and the hours. Mosconi picked on the exhausted promoter like he was a scab. At first, Arnie would hold his cool and let the remarks pass, but eventually there would be a famous blow-up between the two.

These were the days when tuxedo tournaments were in their last throes. Mosconi epitomized these formal affairs and everything about his tux was magnificent and proper. The man was a showcase of style. If you were unfortunate enough to cross his path while wearing a baggy rental tux he would talk to you like a priest addressing a pornographer. His disapproving scowl would follow your entrance across the floor with the repulsed awe of a child watching a worm become bait for the first time.

George Chenier, former World Snooker Champion, was a Canadian who had developed into a very good Straights player. He and Mosconi and I all had the same afternoon off from competition one day, so we had lunch together and wound up spending the afternoon telling stories and listening to Willie expound on the foul judgment of Satin. George left our company that evening in good spirits, looking forward to his match the next day.

As the time for that match approached, we couldn't find George. He was nowhere to be seen and when I asked around it appeared that no one had seen him all day. When I asked Mosconi about him, he said he hadn't seen George either and was concerned because George wasn't the kind of guy to blow off a match. Both of us were concerned enough that we went up to his room to check on him. When we got there we found a 'do not disturb' sign on the door. We pounded on it anyway and got no response.

We saw a maid down the hall and got her to open the door and there in the middle of the room lay George, helpless. Apparently he couldn't reach the door or the phone when he had a stroke and he just fell to the floor and couldn't move.

Well, the stroke was bad enough news for Chenier and his friends, but it also messed up the tournament because it created an empty slot that had to be filled. Satin had to find a stick to go in the empty slot and he invited a hot new player to the tournament, Steve Mizerak. Then, about four days into the tournament, Arnie Risen, the promoter with the money, had a heart attack and died! So Arnie Satin now had to shoulder the entire burden of the tournament on his own.

Meanwhile, on the tournament floor, Mosconi was having a pretty good event. But not playing all the time is going to hurt you. Pool requires repetition and if you don't play regularly you get inconsistent. So one night, Mosconi was playing Weenie-Beanie and having an off night. He would run two balls and miss. It was really embarrassing for him. To make matters worse, there was a fan in the audience who was pulling for Staton and every time Mosconi would miss a ball this guy would yell out, "C'mon Beanie, get something started! Let's get going!" And Beanie, also not having a great performance, would get up, run one or two balls and miss.

So after a while Mosconi got into it with the guy in the audience and he was screaming at him and finally demanded that the guy be thrown out. As Mosconi came to realize after only a few days of competition, he was no longer a force capable of dominating an event. This caused his mood to shift to the dark side and he became worse company with each passing day. In fact, he behaved so badly that Brunswick pulled their sponsorship of him, severing the relationship with the world's greatest player rather than risk any embarrassment by being connected with his potentially devastating behavior.

Mosconi became so insufferable that people were afraid to play him. They didn't want to be subjected to the abuse. One who really didn't want to play him was my roommate, Richie Florence. Richie was in his early twenties then and not at all seasoned in tournament play. The crowds made him self-conscious. When he was scheduled to play Willie, the presence of an audience to amplify the Mosconi mouth was a daunting prospect. Weenie-Beanie saw that Richie was nervous and he went over to him, put his arm around him and said: "Listen, I tell ya' what you gotta do. See that Cocktail Lounge across the street? Go over there and have a martini. Then get one more to go, bring it over here, put it on your table and sip it while you play Mosconi. It'll make your nerves go away, I promise."

So Richie promptly trotted across the street and had nine martinis and brought one back with him to have during the match. He was way too drunk to play Straight Pool. Mosconi beat him 150 to −16. But Richie never did look nervous.

Rooming next door at the tournament was Eddie Taylor. Eddie, who has now been dry for many years, was known to tip a bottle in those days and one morning about 4:30 he called our room and said, "Danny, I'm dying. I'm dying. Call me an ambulance."

So I did. And the ambulance came and took him off to the hospital. Richie and I were standing out there in the dark of the parking lot watching the ambulance wail away from us. Richie turned to me and said, "Man, what a tournament. One guy with a stroke, the promoter up and dies on us, and now our buddy Eddie is in bad shape."

We had to go back to bed and get some sleep. We still had to play our matches that day. We dozed back off about dawn and then at 8 AM the phone rang again. It was Eddie! He was okay and back from the hospital and in his room, but he was already undressed and wanted to know if I'd go get him some ice for his drink.

The tournament was a great success and the place was a sell-out every night. I got to be friends with Peter Faulk, and Fred Astaire would call and ask me to meet him out front so he would have someone to walk in with and not be detained so long with autographs and the like. He was a real nice guy, but a little bit shy and I think he would rather have just been left alone. Willie Mosconi, as Astaire's friend, was also his favorite player. I would sit with Astaire, and

Willie would be playing and throwing one of his tantrums. One of the rules was that you had to sit in your chair while your opponent was playing and Willie just would not do that. He would run all over the place while the other guy played.

The referee was hounding Mosconi to get in his chair. Astaire squirmed in his seat through all of this and got so embarrassed, that he would put his hands in his face and moan. "Oh, God, don't let him act like that. Oh, Willie, please!" And of course Willie couldn't hear any of this and would just keep acting the brat.

All of the problems aside, Richie and I were having a good time. We would stay up late each night, drinking and laughing in our room, and we were a bit noisy, so the manager was getting complaints. He went to the tournament promoters and complained and said that he was going to have to throw us out of our room.

Satin scolded us and we promised to be good and went back to our room that night and partied as hard and loud as ever. A nasty look the next day from the manager inspired me and I made a dummy out of clothes hangers that night and covered it with clothes. Richie and I tied bricks to it, put a full bottle of red ink in it and threw it in the pool so that it looked like a bloody body.

Then we went back to our room and I stood in the door and let go with a few rounds from a starter's gun, a blank pistol. The whole place went nuts. Everybody ran out to the pool, saw the 'body' on the bottom of the pool oozing blood, and called the cops and the rescue squad.

The cops came out in several squad cars and milled around and asked everybody if they'd seen anything or knew who the dead guy was in the water. When a bunch of detectives got there they had the rescue squad put on scuba gear and dive down to get the body. When they surfaced with the clothes hanger dummy, the crowd had a big laugh at their expense and the cops made the manager's life difficult, complaining that they had enough real stuff to mess with and didn't need to be called out to investigate clothes hangers.

On the final night of the tournament they did the tournament room up real fancy and had dinner tables on the floor for the VIP'S. It was a good thing that the VIP's had some food to keep their attention because the final match was terrible. Mosconi's rust had come to full flower and Joe Balsis was completely out of stroke. Neither of them could get any kind of run going. After twenty innings, the score was still only 68 to 64. Finally Balsis got enough momentum going to run 68 balls and win the tournament.

Then Arnie Satin, the remaining live promoter, walked up to Mosconi and reminded him not to leave because they were going to do a trophy presentation for first and second place and they wanted to do it real nice and formal. Mosconi, never fond of finishing second, told Arnie to take the trophy and shove it up his ass. That was the straw that broke the Camel's back. Satin had put up with the crap from Mosconi long enough and he took his coat off, threw it on the floor and turned angrily to Mosconi. "I've heard enough of Willie Mosconi!" He squared off against him and they started sparring.

Legend has expanded this story to the point where the two men traded vicious blows and one of them knocked the other unconscious. But, contrary to the myth, no punches ever landed and bystanders pulled the combatants away from one another pretty quickly.

PLAYING IT STRAIGHT FOR A WHILE

This story has grown so much over the decades that it now falls into the 'dead player' category of legend. That rule has always been that the longer a player is dead, the better he played.

One of the sponsors of the tournament was the owner of a Burbank Italian restaurant and he had arranged with everyone to have the cash available to cash the prize checks from the tournament and have a little party at the restaurant with flowing wine and pasta. So we all wound up over there and all night long players were cashing their checks and everything was great. But Balsis decided to keep his $5,000 check and take it back to Minersville, PA and show it off because, after all, he had beaten Mosconi and that was big!

Eddie Taylor was on his way to Vegas, so he just took his check with him to the Stardust. When Eddie and Joe tried to cash their checks, they bounced because they were drawn on a temporary business account that was already closed. Everyone else had gotten theirs cashed at the restaurant. Eddie never did get his money, but when another group of promoters threw an event the following year, Balsis refused his invitation, citing the $5,000 loss from the previous year. The new group paid Balsis the five grand and he came to their tournament and played.

In the middle of the Satin tournament, I had gotten a call from Hialeah, from the Family Billiard Center and it was Ellie and her lawyers and they were in a panic. "Ted has died. He had a heart attack and he's gone. Danny, you've got to come back and take the room. No one else can run the place." But I had to turn them down. I was in the middle of a twenty-six day tournament and I was winning, so I couldn't just forfeit out.

When I got back to Hialeah, Ellie told me to take the room and run it as if it were my own. And that's what I did and that's when I got all the action with the pool and the girls. I had a standing offer where I had set aside one night per week when I would play a challenger and if they beat me they won a hundred bucks. I put up bleachers and they were filled for these matches. If a bunch of challengers showed up, we would draw a name out of the hat. This brought all the action and top players to my room. Business was tremendous. I could look out of the one-way mirror in my office and see my girlfriends sitting together chatting, waiting to see me. Cheating had become a way of life for me, whether at home in Miami or on the road.

Pam was one of my favorite girls. She worked the Johnston City events selling drinks out of the window between the Show-Bar and the Cue Club. She was gorgeous. She made the move on me, so it was real easy to bed her down and she was fantastic. Like an ice cream cone, she was so delicious. We had something going and she would write me love letters to the Family Billiard Center. I had hired my father to come down from Buffalo to be the day manager and Pam wrote me love letters that she sent to the poolroom so that Francine would never see them. But Dad gathered up the mail and took it home and Francine saw one of the letters on the kitchen counter. That's when everything went south with the marriage.

It was time for the marriage to end. Francine was married, but I wasn't. It really wasn't fair to her at all. When Francine and I split, she packed me meatball sandwiches and I hit the road, leaving the poolroom and family life behind me.

Chapter Eight
THE WHALEN TOURNAMENTS

By 1968 the California tournament scene was largely Fred Whalen. He had a tuxedo-clad invitational every February. Each year at the player's meeting, Fred would give us the exact same lecture. We had to be on our best behavior. Representatives from a big corporation were watching us and they would get involved in sponsoring pool if they liked what they saw. Same story every year. No sponsorships ever came forward.

Fred was nearly 80. He had been one of the Masked Marvels for Coca-Cola in the 20's. Coke used to have a zillion Masked Marvels doing shows in poolrooms. People thought there were only a couple of "Marvels," so the word was that only the best one or two players in the world were Marvels. But Coca-Cola didn't spring for anything that elaborate. They could always find a good local player who lived near where they needed to do a show and get the player to work for them, making a few stops around the area before turning in the mask. It was always one of the best local players that they hired, someone good enough to do a show, but it wasn't like Welker Cochran or Hoppe or Mosconi was out there entertaining the kids with trick shots.

Fred loved the game. He wanted to be involved in it as he grew older and this was how he did it, by having this Straight Pool tournament every February. Each year his event grew in prominence and even Irving Crane made an appearance in the field. Irving always came to a tournament carrying two cue sticks in one of the old square Brunswick cases. Everyone knew he always had two cues and if another player had been forced to sell his cue stick due to pressing economic demands, then Irving, being a nice guy, would lend them one with which to shoot their matches.

The tournament was played in the Elks Building, which had a stage on one end that faced out into the auditorium where Fred had set up seating for the fans, with the tournament table in the middle of the room. At the beginning of each match, the players would be announced and they would come out on the stage from behind the curtain and make their entrance down the stairs to the playing table on the main floor.

One night Johnny Ervolino was borrowing one of Crane's Balabushkas. Johnny needed to use the cue in a match against New Jersey Joe Russo, who later went on to invent the Russo interlocking bridge that you still see in pool rooms everywhere. Russo was a very good player and this match was a grudge deal before the lag even got things started. The day before in a partner One Pocket game, Ervolino was short one barrel and owed that money to Russo, who had still not been paid. These side games were just a little action, a diversion to fill the time between matches. We would draw pills for partners and play One Pocket for $20 a man.

Ervolino played a very determined, aggressive match. He wanted revenge and to prove that he was the superior player. He surged out to a lead that he never intended to surrender. Finally, Johnny needed only 6 or 7 balls to win the match and he played a good safety to stall for a decent out. Russo got up out of his chair, banged in an off-angle combination like it was a hanger, and ran 71 and out to snatch the victory away from him. Russo went over to shake Ervolino's hand and Johnny, very upset at the lost, refused his hand. He swore at him instead and called him a creep. Joe Russo wasn't going to put up with that so he turned to the crowd and said, "Look, who's calling ME a creep!" As he said that, Ervolino had just finished putting Crane's cue back into the case. Without hesitating, he picked up the case and whacked Russo right over the head with it. He hit him so hard it sounded like a shotgun going off. Crane completely freaked out and went running over and grabbed his cues. He never let anyone borrow one of them again for as long as he lived. Russo, more amused by the blow than injured, just walked away; dumbfounded that anyone would actually do something like that.

Irving Crane was always one to watch at tournament play. He took titles very seriously and played as hard as anyone I can remember. But he played too long. I could never beat Irving Crane when he was in his prime. Even when he was in his forties and fifties he owned me. He owned everybody—he was that good at Straights. I only started to best him when age finally began to strip him of his abilities. Time is the one guy you can't beat in this game.

At the very end, the dementia or whatever it was, would surface from time to time with Irving and in embarrassing ways. He would be in a tournament and get out of line a bit on a break shot and pick up the cue ball and move it over an inch or so to get the angle he wanted for the shot. The referee would call 'Foul' and Irving would turn around and say something like: "It's okay, I'm just knocking 'em around." Then I or another friend would have to go up and say,

"Irv, this is a tournament. You're in a tournament match and that was a foul. Now go take your chair!" And if you said it in the right voice he would get a blank look on his face, then understand and go sit down, embarrassed. And it made everyone feel so bad.

In one match I remember, he had already done that once in an earlier inning and then he was shooting along and missed the ten-ball. And he just kept shooting. The referee was going: "Mr. Crane, sir, you have missed and must take your chair now." And Irv turned around and said, "It's okay, I'm just shooting 'em some." And so for the second time I had to go out and tell my old friend that it was a tournament match and he needed to take his chair and let his opponent come to the table.

When he understood, his eyes hung on mine for a moment, enough time only for a memory to flash, and my heart was seared with the sight of his walk back to the chair. As he sat down, the hushed chuckles from the audience reached him and his shoulders slumped from their blow. When I think of it now, my jaw clenches and my eyes close. It is a moment that will always haunt me.

But in 1968, Crane was still great and sharp as a tack. He was with us as was an entire squad of new faces. This was the year that Ron Roper from California was invited to the event. Ron was a good-looking twenty-four year old with long blonde hair who dressed immaculately. One night, he was on center stage playing his match and stretched out across the table to get to his next shot. As he leaned out for the shot, his long blonde hair caught on the table lights and his flowing locks came off and tumbled to the floor. The man was bald as a rock. He went from Fabio to Mr. Clean in front of the whole world. It was such a surprising moment that the entire room felt sorry for him and fell silent.

He never showed any signs of being shook. He calmly bent down, got his wig, and went up on the stage to stand behind the curtain to rearrange his hairpiece. Then he re-emerged, came down the stairs to new applause, and continued his game. He ran fifty or sixty balls when he resumed his inning.

The promoter of these tournaments, Fred Whalen, was an interesting guy. They say he made his living traveling around the country hooking up with local pool players and entering them into a profitable proposition. He would ask them if they knew anyone locally who liked to do a little booking.

This proposition went to the heart of the law that says that with any type of hustle, you can only beat someone who is trying to beat you. If they aren't trying to get something for nothing, then they'll get shy or scared and won't stay with the deal long enough for you to get to the payoff. You have to have a mark who owns enough greed to fuel the deal.

Whalen was a nice guy who loved pool players and he always took care of them, but he was supposed to be the best at this one particular gaff. He had a big house in Hollywood that people said was funded with this ploy. This is how it worked:

The key was to find someone who wanted to be a bookmaker. The local pool player contact would have nominated someone they knew who wanted some easy booking action and would have schooled the mark on the idea that there was a local doctor who had approached him about making some small daily bets on the ponies.

Whalen would plant himself in the local hospital with a stethoscope, a white jacket and padded shoes—the whole doctor deal. Key to the bookie, was the info that the bets would be small, just five and ten dollar action. Nothing a bookie could get hurt on, so there was nothing to worry about. Since horse action is what every bookie wants, it would be hard to resist the temptation.

The mark was told to go to the hospital and meet the doctor in the waiting room. The doctor (Whalen) supposedly had a partner, who did all this bookmaking previously; but the partner had died and the doctor needed a new bookie to handle his action and keep things cool. A reputable doctor could not have it known he was involved in this sort of thing. The fledgling bookie was made to feel a part of a minor conspiracy and the intrigue added to his excitement.

The doctor would come into the meeting with a bag full of betting slips and all the money required to cover the bets thrown into the bag. The bookie was to pick up the bag at the end of the day, figure all the bets up, do a tally and get back to the doctor the next day to settle up and collect the next day's bets. It all sounded so simple.

When the mark went in to collect the bag, the doctor would sit with him and they would talk for a while about how the bookie would do the tally and how they would cut up the money and what percentages would be used and just chat a little in pleasant conversation.

While they were chatting there would be announcements and pages coming over the hospital PA and the doctor would occasionally take notes on his little pad, the kind that doctors always carry

THE WHALEN TOURNAMENTS

around. What the mark had no way of knowing, was that Whalen was listening to the announcements for a voice code and the notes he was making were actually new betting slips that reflected the results of races being run while he and the sucker were talking.

Whalen had an accomplice out at the racetrack, who would get the results and call the hospital and ask for a visitor to be paged. If the PA announced: "Would Mr. John Applewhite please call his office," then that told Whalen that a certain horse had won a certain race. The 'notes' the doctor was taking was a new bet being formulated, a long-odds parlay phoned in by the accomplice.

So as the conversation ended and the doctor handed the bag over to the bookie, he would slip one more bet in with the parlay on it and the deal was done. At the end of the day, the bookie would be tallying everything up, losing $5 here and winning $10 here and it all looked fine, until he got to the slip with the parlay. Now the way a parlay works is you bet say five bucks on an 18 - 1 shot and win. In the second race you take all that you just won (18 X $5 = $90) and bet on the next long-shot winner, say a 14 -1 deal. Now your $90 gets multiplied by 14 and you have $1,260. The odds are used to turn a small bet into a big winner.

And that's how the Whalen tournaments were rumored to be funded. He played the doctor role in cities all over the country and used the money he 'won' to pay out nice purses to the players. His checks always cashed.

It was also through one of these West Coast swings that I got to meet Joe Namath. I had gotten a call from one of the owners of a nightclub out there called "The Factory," who asked if I would come out and play some Straight Pool with a friend of his named Joe. The Factory was a very hot spot at the time, a place where the stars went to drink and relax, and he said they would make me an honorary lifetime member if I would come and play.

I was to play Joe a game of Straight Pool with a handicap of my one hundred points to his thirty-five and they were laying four hundred dollars to two hundred on the money. So I had to out-point him by nearly three to one, which wasn't a big deal, unless Joe could string racks together, which he couldn't.

I was very comfortably ahead at the end of the game, when Joe Namath walked into the room. The two Joes were friends, as Namath came over and shook Joe's hand and said his hello's to him before he turned to greet others in the room. By this time, I had finished out the final rack and was waiting to see if we would play again or if that was all the entertainment the group desired for the day.

Namath spoke up and told his friend: "Play him another game and this time I'll tell you what to do. I'll be your coach." Being a bit of a wise guy I replied, "If he promises to listen, I'll spot him ten more balls." That drew a chuckle from the crowd and we played another game with Namath guiding my opponent. He had no idea of what to do. He steered poor Joe wrong time after time and missed obvious opportunities to score. I wound up beating the guy by a wider margin than I had before.

After the final ball dropped, Namath grabbed me by the arm and started shaking me, playing to the crowd, I suppose. I said, "Hey, wait a minute. I'm not very big, but I hit hard and I don't want to be roughed up, so we need to quit this." He knew that he had stepped over the line of proper civility, so he put his arm around me and replied, "Hey, can I buy you a drink over here?"

We wound up sitting at a table drinking burgundy wine all night long and watching the beautiful girls as they came and went from the club. This was the era of the mini-skirt and girls playing pool in mini-skirts was a marvelous spectator sport. When they bent to shoot, they had to pretend that they don't know they were displaying all their wares.

During the course of the night, Namath made a statement that I just let pass because it was so ludicrous. The Jets had been a losing team and he said: "Next year the Jets are going all the way. We will win the Super Bowl." I just let it slide, not wishing to speak a truth that might be rude. How prophetic he was. The next year the Jets went to the Super Bowl; Namath made his famous guarantee of a win; and they beat the Colts for the title!

Chapter Nine
LOST DOGS AND LOSERS

One of the tournaments that I just had to attend every year was the World Straight Pool Championships in Los Angeles. I still had the station wagon that I had used for the ovenware sales; a vehicle that could carry enough ovenware to get me through a good day of sales. There was plenty of room for my cues and bags and even room left for some friends.

I traveled then with a male pit bull named 'Fink' and an Airedale named 'Torra.' I always loved dogs and they made traveling a lot easier. I'd throw a tape in the 8-track, settle back in the driver's seat, and talk and sing to the dogs and it didn't matter if you had to drive sixteen hours straight, the dogs made it fun and were always the best company, because they never disagreed with what you said. You could tell them anything and they would just grin and stick their heads back out the window. A little water, a little kibble and a frequent rub around the ears was all they ever wanted. And when they put the bite on you it's free. Great friends.

We had gotten almost all the way through Arizona on our way to the tournament. It was two in the morning and on this highway there was nothing but myself and my dogs and the light from about a billion stars. When I stopped to let the dogs stretch, I would lean back on my car and look into the heavens and it was amazing. In the desert, there's no light to interfere with the stars. No streetlamps, no glow from the city, no porch lights, nothing. So when the moon isn't out, the heavens look like a black floor that has been dusted with pinpoints of silver. There are so many of them that the little pinpoints almost touch each other. The Milky Way spreads out across the whole hemisphere like a big white ribbon. It's gorgeous.

And when your car dies out there, it is a vivid reminder that you are literally all alone and a long way from any help. For a New Yorker, I was trapped in a very hostile atmosphere. I'd rather have been alone in a Philly biker bar with a 'kick me' sign on my back than out there in the desert.

Just as the worry was starting to set in for real, I saw headlights coming over the horizon. In a few minutes, an ancient pick-up truck came lumbering down the highway and stopped by my car. It was an old couple going home and they told me there was a town about thirty-five miles down the road with a garage.

The old guy got out and dragged a long chain out of the back of his truck and he got down and hooked it up to the frame of my car. The two of them towed me all the way to this little garage and they acted like 'of course this is how you treat strangers.' They were two of the nicest folks I had ever met. By now, it was around three in the morning and the old guy went right over to a pay phone on the corner and called up the mechanic whose name was on the garage and woke him up and ran him through the story of how I broke down out on the highway and all and the mechanic got right up out of the bed, got dressed, and came on in to start work on my car!

After the mechanic took his initial look, he said the water pump had gone out and it would take about five hours to get a new one and get it in the car. Plus, the car overheated and warped the heads, so there was going to be a lot of work involved and I knew that wasn't going to be cheap.

By now, dawn had forced the sun back to work and I was stranded in this little town, Victorville, just across the California border from Arizona. As luck would have it, there was a little bar across the road and as the mechanic began to remove the heads, I saw the lights go on. After an hour of sweating the life or death situation with the engine, the mechanic said he could save her, so my stomach began to demand attention. I left the dogs in the wagon while he worked and set out across the street for the bar.

It had already gotten warm, even though it was still only mid-morning. When I entered the bar, the cool air gave my spirit a little second wind and I sat down and ordered a beer and a sandwich. Of course, there was a little bar table in there and people were playing on it and having a good time so I put my quarter down on the rail to get in line to play. It was the usual bar deal. They were playing 'King of the Mountain' where the loser sits down and the winner stays at the table. Once I got up to shoot, it became pretty obvious that I wasn't going to be sitting down until I got tired, but all the guys seemed to enjoy the challenge, so I was having a good time knocking balls around with the townsfolk. After a while, a couple in their 30's introduced themselves and said they really enjoyed watching me play and that they had a little spread just outside of town.

When they heard of my car plight, they said I should come out to their ranch and relax a while and the mechanic could call me when the car was ready and I wouldn't have to kill time in the bar. So I got my dogs and we drove out to their place in the foothills.

There was a pool table in their game room, so I put on a little show for them and we became good friends. We passed the time over a few beers and a few games and after lunch the garage called and said my car was ready. My new friends drove me back to town. I shook his hand and gave her a hug and I was on the road again.

The dogs must have been kept awake by the work on the car because as soon as we cleared the city limits and were in the desert again, they conked out on me and Fink was snoring like an old wino. I was considering my good fortune to not only have found that mechanic, but also to have been helped by the old couple and to have been welcomed into the home of strangers. I was only about a hundred miles short of L.A. when the car dropped a bunch of metal on the highway and the engine fell silent. But my luck was still holding a bit, as I was atop a hill when the car suffered its stroke and at the bottom of the hill was a gas station that I could coast down to so at least I wasn't stuck in the desert heat with the dogs.

But I had a real problem. The last repair shop had drained my financial resources and this round would cost another six or seven hundred bucks. No way did I have that kind of cash. So the mechanic there gave me a ride a few blocks to a real nice kennel where I could board the dogs and not need to worry about their safety or comfort. He told me he would fix the car and hold it until I could come back and bail it out.

The kennel was one of those plush ones where they walk the dogs and play with them and every dog has his own private little sleeping hut and run. So my two pets were now on vacation and their spa treatment was costing me seven bucks a day. In addition to the fact that I missed my dogs and wanted them back with me, there was the added incentive of fifty bucks a week and the meter would keep running until I came back and got them. I needed to get to L.A. and do well enough to come back to this little burg and bail out my dogs and my ovenware wagon.

By late afternoon my thumb got a bite and I caught a ride to L.A. Suitcase in one hand, cue stick in the other, when I crawled out of the car in L.A. I was the poster boy for quiet desperation. I had to keep my cool as that's required in my line of work, but I also needed to raise some fast cash.

This was the year of a real bad California earthquake. They said it was a 7.8 magnitude at the epicenter and it shook the place up real good. I had gotten a room on the ground floor of the motel where everyone was staying and I was sleeping about five the next morning when the ground got up like it was going to leave. I could barely walk across the floor to get to the window. I felt like the foredeck guy on a boat in a bad storm that has to go way out front on the boat and set a sail. I was being bounced around like one of those little men on an electric football game.

From the window I could see the water in the pool being sloshed around and coming out all over the deck. Later, I found out that some of the guys in the tournament were staying in a hotel downtown and they couldn't stand upright at all. They had to crawl down eight dark flights of stairs on their bellies like snakes.

There were aftershocks for the next four or five days. You would be playing in the tournament room and the chandelier above the table would start swinging. Steve Cook had hooked himself with a pocket teat and was cussing himself when one of the aftershocks moved his ball enough to clear the pocket so he could continue his run.

Some of the players, even the undefeated ones like Cook and Dallas West, were so disconcerted by the quake and the aftershocks that kept coming that they left and went home. They gave up with both barrels still loaded so they could get back to ground that didn't argue with their feet.

I figured Irving Crane would leave. His disposition always leaned a little towards nervousness and I figured him for the next train out of town. But he appeared unfazed. He still took his morning walk every day as usual. He had suffered polio as a kid and he had a little gimp to his walk, but he knew the value of exercise and he walked every day no matter where he was. He told me that whenever one of the tremors hit he would go grab a tree. He said the roots would hold the ground together so he didn't have to worry about being swallowed up by some fissure. It didn't bother him at all.

This is the same guy that would never fly. He would take a train every year from Rochester all the way to L.A. just for this tournament. It would take him four travel days in each direction. So it was pretty obvious to everyone that the Deacon didn't like to fly. And in those days, those fears were a lot better founded, because planes really did have a lot more problems with gravity than they do now. They didn't have the electronics of today and the aircraft weren't nearly as sophisticated. I can remember planes that crashed because their engines fell off, so Irving wasn't alone when he chose not to take the risk.

Pool players are quite aware that pool is a game where your confidence and attitude play a big part in how well you play. You have to be confident to play well and you never want to show any weakness of any kind. No chinks in the armor for an opponent to explore. So Irving and many others of the day put up this ironclad exterior that denied any weaknesses to the opponent.

One day Irving and I were in the bar at the hotel and I asked him why he was afraid to fly. I knew I had to play him to get through the brackets and I might as well send him upstairs to his pillow for the night with the knowledge that I was aware he was human and capable of fear. Now, this may not provide any advantage during our eventual match, but it wouldn't hurt me and I've seen championships determined by one ball. I find it difficult to define a one ball advantage or how to create one, but I think the mind shift resulting from just the comment about airplanes could justify that margin. So I laid it out on the table to see if I could get him to flinch a bit.

He had seen this pitch come across his plate before. It was to his advantage to blow off the airplane and focus my attention on his strength, which was not only his uncanny skill, but also his timing and his patience in waiting for the right situation to take the proper risk and have it reward him with victory. So he just grinned at me when I asked him about it and he said: "Oh, I'm not afraid to fly at all. I'm just never in a big hurry."

Now I had to go upstairs for the night and wonder if he had just told me that my playing pace was too hurried or that I sometimes jumped up on a shot. I tried to plant a seed of doubt and got it tossed back like the light off a mirror. Irving was a pretty crafty character. By the time I got to know him well, there just wasn't much that he hadn't already seen.

I finished seventh in the tournament that year and my prize money was about twelve hundred dollars. But I hadn't done as well at the track betting windows as I had hoped and I was really in a fix. That year the track crew that consisted of Joe Balsis, Cicero Murphy, Jersey Red and his wife, and myself hadn't found many winners. The only positive was that I became friends during this time with Balsis. I never cared for Joe until I saw him with a handful of betting slips. When I discovered that he was just another degenerate gambler, he became like a long lost brother to me.

But my financial ditch was deepening. My dogs were still living it up at the doggy spa and my car was fixed, but I couldn't afford the repair bill. Plus, the tournament at the Stardust started in a week and I was flat busted.

Whalen had given me some advances against my winnings to take to the track. This became painful when I went to collect my prize money. He figured up the advances, subtracted them from the twelve hundred I had won and said: "Okay, Danny, here's the buck I owe you." I was standing there stunned when I heard someone mention that Bob Ogburn was in Bellflower, just down the road. Bob was an old friend and great road partner and I figured he could be my salvation. We would make some money in Bellflower and then team up to go to Vegas. I found a couple of guys heading south and caught a ride out of L.A.

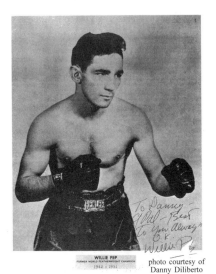

photo courtesy of
Danny Diliberto

Willie Pep

photo courtesy of Mike Shamos

DANNY DILIBERTO

One of the hottest players in billiards today. Recently won the Johnson City
championship. Before that he finished
second in the Billiards Congress of America tournament, a double elimination test.
He's 32 years old, married and lives in
Miami. He was a surprise 5th-place winner
in last year's world championships with a
12-7 record. Gave up promising careers in
boxing and baseball to concentrate on billiards.

Danny in the news.

photo courtesy of Danny Diliberto

Danny and Sugar Ray Robinson

photo courtesy of Danny Diliberto

Pete Margo, Fred Astaire, and Danny

photo courtesy of Mike Shamos

Danny as a
young player

photo courtesy of Danny Diliberto

Danny with artwork.

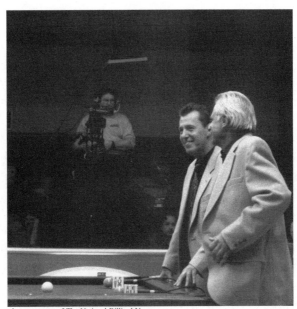

photo courtesy of The National Billiard News

Danny doing commentary with Jimmy Mataya

Danny in action.

Hubert Cokes
(Daddy Warbucks)

Shake N Bake
(Edgar White)

Buddy Hall

photo courtesy of The National Billiard News

photo courtesy of The National Billiard News

Boston Shorty
(Larry Johnson)

U. J. Puckett

photo courtesy of The
National Billiard News

Louie Roberts

photo courtesy of The National Billiard News

Danny Jones

photo courtesy of The National Billiard News

Bill Staton
(Weenie Beanie)

photo courtesy of The National Billiard News

Jimmy Reid

Larry Liscotti

Ed Kelly

Grady Mathews

Jimmy
Fusco

Jimmy
Mataya

Wade
Crane

Ronnie Allen

photo courtesy of The National Billiard News

Richie Florence

photo courtesy of The National Billiard News

Steve Mizerak and Luther Lassiter

photo courtesy of The National Billiard News

**Joe Caldwell
& Bugs Rucker**

Larry Hubbard

B. Stigall & Richie Ambrose

photo courtesy of Danny Diliberto

"LEARN FROM THE BEST"

| Jimmy
Fusco | Wade
Crane | Kim
Davenport | Jimmy
Reid | Larry
Liscotti | Jim
Rempe | Danny
Diliberto | Larry
Hubbard | Mike
Sigel | Nick
Varner | Jimmy
Mataya |

Chapter Ten
AT THE PALACE

This was not my first trip to Palace Billiards. A Straight Pool player named Vern Peterson owned the room and it was there that I had first met a young kid named Keith McCready. It was in the late sixties and there was high-stakes action going twenty-four hours a day. Stakehorses filled every chair and incredible gambling went on there for over a year. Keith was in on the action at night and sleeping under the tables in the daytime. He was a skinny, pimple-faced twelve-year-old who, due to his skills, was accepted into the adult world of racks and payouts.

Keith loved pool and gambling. He would go to the horse track with the other players and they would have to place his bets for him because he wasn't old enough to place his own. I started worrying about this kid I saw sleeping under the tables and I was wondering why he wasn't in school. So one day I cornered him and asked about that.

"Keith," I said. "I'm not trying to stick my nose into your business, but why aren't you in school getting an education?"

"They kicked me out," he said.

"Kicked you out? Why did they kick you out, Keith?"

"For having too much money."

"Too much money? They kicked you out for having too much money? Why would they kick you out for that?"

"I don't know. I just asked my gym teacher to hold my cash one day because I was afraid to leave it in my locker; I thought it could be stolen. So the gym teacher sort of smiled at me and said, 'Sure I'll hold your cash." Then he asked me how much I had. I pulled twelve grand out of my pocket and they kicked me out for having too much money."

The main game that everyone played in Bellflower was a great gambling game called Pay Ball. It was played with six balls on a big twelve-foot snooker table with real tight, round pockets. Every ball was a money ball and the six-ball carried a bonus of double the value of all the other balls for being the last ball. It was common for a group of four or five guys to be playing 20-40 Pay Ball, so all the balls were worth twenty dollars, except the six and it was worth forty. If you happened to run out, which was real tough, that paid double again so a run would catch two-hundred-eighty dollars from every player. If you were playing in a group with four other sticks you pulled in over a grand for running six balls!

Keith, at twelve years old, was so good that he broke the game two weekends in a row and got everybody's cash. Against the best players in the country! Ronnie Allen lived out there and really liked the Pay Ball games. The games would go on for four or five days sometimes and some players would stay in the whole time if they could get their chemicals right. Others, like Ronnie, would get in on the first day, win a little, get out and go home and get some sleep and then come back the next day and get in again and win more. He would do this day after day, so each day he was fresh and playing guys who hadn't slept in days.

One day Ronnie came in to play and there were four guys in the game and one of them was Richie Florence, who had gone broke, but was playing on a system of markers with the others at the table and I was keeping the books for him. Every time a ball was made I would note who Richie owed and how much. This is really rare in gambling. I mean, the guy might die overnight and you would never get your money, but they were letting him play on these markers.

When Ronnie came in, he declared himself in the game. When you did that, you had to sit out one more game and then the players would draw new pills for playing order and you would get in the rotation according to the pill you drew. So Ronnie came in and said: "Okay, I'm in. Draw me a pill when it's time."

Richie knew Ronnie wouldn't accept the markers he was using for money and replied, "No you're not, Ronnie, you can't play." Plus, Richie didn't like the idea that Ronnie kept going home and getting rest and food while he continued to tire at the table. Ronnie stormed up to him: "Nobody bars me from a game!" and they got into a shouting match. Finally Richie cut loose and hit Ronnie square on the jaw with a left hook. Ronnie fell back on a table and got back up a little groggy. "Richie, anyone who hits me clean and doesn't put me down, can't whip me. Let's go outside."

They went outside and after about ten feet Ronnie spun and threw a sucker-punch haymaker that missed by a mile. Not even close. The swing and a miss caused them both to break out laughing and they went back inside as friends and stayed friends from that day forward. Ronnie didn't try to enter the game until Richie went home the next day.

AT THE PALACE

That was all several years previous and this time when I walked into the Palace I was as broke as I had ever been in my life. But standing there in the back of the room I could see big Bob and I knew that if he was there, my fortunes would improve. Bob was a slow moving Southerner who just loved to gamble. He was a bit strange; always saying that money was dirty and that he felt cleansed when he was broke, but Bob Ogburn was never out of action.

Right away he took the bloom off my rose. His first words were: "Oh, Danny, things are bad. The action here is gone. I'm trapped without enough action to win a ticket out of town!" And that's how it was. The action that had been so heavy just a few years before had now moved on to another city. Action never hangs in one place forever. After a while the suits find out about it and then the cops see it as a crusade and the politicians see it as a given to rid the town of such evil and then everyone just gets on their horse and rides to the next place down the line. And the pale riders had already passed this way and gone. There wasn't enough action left to back a shoeshine. The Pay Ball game had degenerated to quarter stakes and the torrents of money had trickled to a whisper of their former glory.

Even the motel up the street where the players once stayed had soured. It had been beaten for rooms so often that it became unbeatable. You had to pay by noon each day in cash or your stuff would be on the street. No excuses. Cash every day or the locks changed. It was twenty dollars a day and Bob was having trouble just staying in his room and keeping a can of Spam on the table. It was a great day when he could get a couple of hamburgers and a six-pack and just relax in the room watching late movies.

My heart was fast desperate again. Between us over the next few days, we really struggled just to get by. The Stardust tournament was looming and we couldn't afford to miss it. In our business, when you get a chance at a big takedown, you have to go for it. It's not like there will be another one next week. And here we were so broke that we couldn't afford the gas to get there, much less the entry fee or hotel money.

Then one day our luck started to shift. We both had a good day scuffling in the poolroom and after we splurged on the luxury of hamburgers and beer and paid for our beds, we still had thirty dollars left between us. This was the first folding money we'd seen since I arrived. But it was still just spit in the wind compared to what we needed to fund the Vegas venture.

I said to Bob, "Man, let me call this girl I know and borrow her car. Then let's take the thirty bucks and go to Santa Anita. At least we got a shot. Right now we got no shot." So that's what we did. We borrowed the girl's VW and went to the track and picked out two daily doubles that both revolved around one horse we liked.

On a daily double you have to pick the first two races to win. We based ours on one long- shot horse named Johnny Do Well. We had two daily doubles based on this shot and he won the first race. In fact, he paid $53.80 to win! So we had two daily doubles still alive when the second race started. One would pay us a little over seventeen hundred if it came in and the other one fifty-six hundred!

We had been suffering for so long that this seemed like great wealth. Even though the bigger payoff eluded us, we still won the other one and had over seventeen hundred dollars to get us to Las

AT THE PALACE

Vegas. Once there, we could get the cash we needed to get my dogs and car out of hock.

We were on our way out of Santa Anita with our grubstake when we ran into Ronnie Allen. Without so much as a 'howdy-do,' he launched into a monologue on how he's got the nuts on this bet in the next race because there was a horse coming up that would blow the doors off everyone else on the track. He said he had an inside line to some guy that lived on the ranch where this horse trained, and that the horse was dusting every other horse on the farm. Ronnie said he was absolutely robbing the windows on this one and that it was like money already in the bank account. We looked at the board and the line was 25-1. Then, on the first flash, the horse went to 3-1, so it was obvious right away that a lot of big money, and that means smart money, was riding this horse. There was a lot of cash out there talking and it was saying that it agreed with what Ronnie was doing.

What else could we do? We put seventeen hundred on the horse to win. I pushed that whole wad through the bars and put the slip in my pocket. At the top of the stretch our horse was coasting along with a six-length lead. Smiles all around. The horse had finally gone off at 7-2 and we stood to win over five thousand dollars. We could go to Vegas in a freaking limousine if we wanted.

Then another horse broke from the pack and began a charge like you have never seen. It looked like the horse had rockets strapped to his ass or something the way he moved up. Even with the huge lead our horse had, this horse was able to overtake him at the wire and win by a nose. Bob and I were broke again. Vegas, two hundred miles away, might as well have been in Russia.

On the way back to the Palace in the VW, I remembered that someone told me Ed Kelly was living in California, and I thought that they said Hollywood. It turned out he was living with a black guy named Rudy and he was as colorful a guy as Ed was. He was a part-time pimp and part-time whatever else he needed to be to raise cash and he loved to gamble and play pool.

So I gave Ed a call and laid out all my cards. I'm broke, the Stardust is happening and my dogs are in jail. He said, "Hey, no problem, come on over and I'll set you up with a couple hundred stake to get you going." Well, that was great, as that would be enough to get to the Stardust.

When we met with Ed, he greeted us like long-lost family and right away handed us the cash we needed. Then he asked if we wanted to go to dinner at Sneaky Pete's restaurant on Sunset Blvd. This is the place Johnny Carson and Ed McMahon would visit when they came out to do shows in California in the days when they did the *Tonight* show from New York. Sometimes Johnny would get up and play the drums and Ed McMahon would sing.

We all went to Sneaky Pete's and had a great meal with wine before dinner, wine with dinner, and wine after dinner. It was a great time, three guys sharing stories and laughs and good food and wine. As we were enjoying our final brandies, the waiter brought the tab and when I checked the bill, I saw that we had just ingested the entire loan. We hadn't even gotten out of the city limits with it.

We left the restaurant and drove west on Sunset where it becomes a little deserted, which was a good thing as we were too

AT THE PALACE

drunk to be driving anyway. I was still driving the borrowed VW and suddenly the alcohol hit Kelly and he started acting up the way he sometimes would under the effects of booze and he started going wild in the back seat, kicking the doors and slamming the windows with his fists. I tried to calm him down, but when he persisted, I began to really worry that he was going to do some damage to the car and I would have to fix it. I finally stopped the car and threw him out on the road. He had loaned us our stake, eaten it away with us, and now stood shaking his fist at me while doing drunken pirouettes as I drove away. Funny how the Mandela turns and things that begin right side up seem to finish upside down.

The next morning, Ogburn and I didn't have a prayer between us. But neither did we have anything to lose, so we packed our stuff and headed down to the highway. We stuck our thumbs out and within half an hour, a car with two pool players headed to the Stardust pulled up and delivered us straight to the door of the Casino just four hours later.

We couldn't check in without cash, so we checked our luggage with the bellman and headed to the practice room. First guy I saw was Daddy Warbucks hitting some balls around. He saw me come in and said, "Diliberto, play me some 100 to 50 and I'll play you for four hundred a game".

Well, Warbucks had to be near 80 by now, so I figured I had to take a shot at this. But I was penniless. I could toss an airball at him, but if I lost, this was not the least dangerous man on the planet to insult with an unexpected debt. Bill Staton happened to overhear the conversation between Warbucks and myself and pulled me aside: "Danny, just think. How many innings do you need to get a hundred balls and how many does he need to get fifty? You've got this covered easily." So I called his bluff and told him if it was such a steal then he should stake it. I had to pull a bluff on someone and at least I thought Beanie could win here.

Which he did. Beanie staked it and the game was on. I played Hubert and beat him two games. We won eight hundred, and half of that was mine and half was Staton's. As we were splitting up the cash, a guy named Meathead from Jackson, Tennessee, walked into the scene. This guy was a real big gambler, a big drinker, a braggart and a real tough talker who in reality was just a sweetheart of a guy who would give money to a stranger if it was needed.

I had gambled with Meathead before and he came up and wanted 10-8 and the breaks in One Pocket. So I consulted with Beanie and he was worried. "I don't know Danny. I played him 9-8 last night and it was really tough. That break can really get you. But if you feel good about it take the eight hundred and shoot at it."

Meathead and I played four hundred a game all night long and when dawn broke through the windows I had eight thousand of his dollars in my pocket. He was broke and had to quit. All night long he had been paying me with black chips and I had this great big bag of chips and he had nothing left. As was customary in those days, I invited him to a meal and we had a nice breakfast together downstairs in the restaurant.

We were destroying some eggs and bacon and just chatting along and I said to him, "Y'know, Meathead, I only know you as Meathead.

I've gambled with you for years and bumped up against you on the road and I have never heard your name."

He looked at me and said, "Name's Bolivar Cotton."

I said "Nice having breakfast with you, Meathead." And he shook his head up and down and then got up and walked out of the Stardust. I've never seen him since.

That tournament I won about four thousand, but I lost that as well as Meathead's money to the Stardust before the thing was over. You can never come out ahead at a casino tournament. You have to get lucky too many times. This thing lasted three weeks and there was no way to avoid the tables the whole time. When you left the tournament to go to your room you had to pass craps tables, black-jack tables, poker tables and the roulette wheel.

Someone said they ought to invent horse blinders for the pool players, so we could get past the casino to our rooms. But no one would have used them. We all left those tournaments broke. What the Casino didn't lift, the bite did. It was impossible to leave Vegas with money in your pocket. We all suffered from the same sickness.

One night before I went broke I got lucky. I won a couple of grand at craps. At the Stardust in those days you could have a nice room for sixty-five a night and be inside, but the cheaper rooms were all outside in a row like a motel with the doors all opening to the parking lot. These blocks of rooms were named after planets and carried names like Mercury and Venus.

In March, Vegas can be very cold and this year it was brutal. You had to leave the casino and go outside to get to your room and the walk was like walking to the South Pole. It was a long way to our block of rooms. It must have been three hundred yards or so.

This night, after I scored the two grand at craps, Larry Liscotti and I braced for the walk to the room. The temperature was right at freezing and the wind was blowing like Louis Armstrong. A frigid gale took our breath when we opened the Casino door and started toward the pool and our rooms beyond.

I can't tell you how cold that pool looked. It looked as deadly as a gun. So for grins as we walked by it I said to Liscotti, "Y'know, seeing you dive off the diving board and into that pool tonight would easily be worth two hundred to me."

Liscotti never even hesitated. He headed straight to the ladder of the diving board, fully clothed, clambered up and did a pretty good swan dive into the pool. When he surfaced, he came out of that water like he had been shot from a cannon. I don't know how he got his body to rise straight up out of the water and onto the deck like that, but he was standing soaked in icy water and the wind was cutting him apart.

He was staring at me with tiny little frozen eyes and I handed him the money. "Larry," I said, "I had a good night tonight. I was going to give you the money anyway."

Liscotti looked me straight in the eye and said, "That's okay, I was going to dive in the pool anyway."

As I said, at the end of the tournament, I was broke again. Broke in Las Vegas with no car and my dogs were still running the kennel meter and the mire I was in, just kept getting deeper. The next morning a fellow I'd seen at the tournament came up to me: "Y'know Danny, if we can scrape together three hundred, we can go on the road and make some dough. I got a good car, you can play pool and I can do what I do and I do something real well."

"I got rules." I told him, "I don't get involved in anything that could put me in jail or get me killed."

"No problem," he said, "No problem at all. What I do may be illegal, but you won't be involved and it's real tough to get caught at it in the first place. But you won't be involved anyway. Now, how do we get the three hundred?"

Just then I saw Billy Incardona coming out of the elevator. We went over and borrowed the three hundred from Billy who didn't even ask if it was a loan or a bite. In short order we were in my new partner's car and headed out of the oasis. This fellow was known as 'Superstroke,' and what he did so well was shortchange people. That's why we had to have the three hundred.

Out in the desert in Superstroke's T-Bird, I arranged the money for his use. The three hundred was converted to three fifties and one hundred and fifty singles. These were arranged into three groups with the fifty on top and twenty-four singles beneath the fifty.

Then, when we got to the first town with a drugstore, Stroke went in to work. First he would make sure that the checkout person was someone who looked pretty innocent. His favorite was always high school kids on a summer job. He avoided middle-aged guys like the plague because they might have seen similar work before.

If the clerk looked doable he would go pick up some tooth-paste or shoe polish and go up to pay for it. His trunk already looked like a drugstore, filled with toothpaste and razor blades and stuff, but these little items were just the excuse he used to get in front of the clerk and begin interacting with the cash register.

He would take his little purchase to the clerk and ask, "Hey, do you need ones?" Well, of course every retail store can always use ones. Folks pay with tens and twenties and the ones go out the door quickly. So the clerk almost always said, "Sure."

He would tell the clerk that he had twenty-five ones that she can have and that he would use them to pay for his $1.25 purchase. He would search his pockets for the ones he had promised. He would look in his pants pocket, then pat down his back pockets, look in his wallet, pat his shirt, and then say, "Oh, never mind. I can't find 'em, here." And he would hand her a fifty.

She would make the change and give him back $48.75. Then, as he was putting up his change he would say, "Oh, here they are," and come out with the ones asking, "Do you still want 'em?" And he would hand over the twenty-four ones and the cashier would hand him a twenty and a five. The clerk would count the ones and come up with only twenty-four. Stroke would look real concerned and go," Are you sure? I know there was twenty-five there."

So the money would be counted again, maybe twice, to make as much time as possible pass after getting the twenty and the five. When the clerk finally 'convinced' Stroke that there were only twenty-four bills there he would say, "Oh, okay, here's a twenty, a five and a one, just gimme back the fifty."

And the innocent little things would hand him that fifty every time. He called it 'winning' twenty-five dollars and could go from store to store until he had earned his nut for the day. He did it every-where. Restaurants, drugstores, grocery stores, everywhere. I didn't like him doing it when I was around, but that didn't stop him. He wanted me to watch because he thought it would impress me. I pre-ferred it when he would drop me at the poolroom and I could go do my thing while he was out alone with his act.

After a couple of days of moving from town to town looking for enough of a score to bail out the dogs and my car, we wound up in Oklahoma City. I stopped into a poolroom and found a player who hung around there named Norman Hitchcock. Norman made a good living defrocking road players and I knew it.

Norman had aged a bit, but he could still play very well. The man had seen so much Nine Ball that there was nothing you could do to surprise him. No matter what you pulled he had seen it before. We set up a game and when the poolroom closed at midnight, I had made my nut for the day and had some good pocket stuffing to boot.

As I was putting my cue up a young guy in wire spectacles walked up to me and, I swear, he didn't look as if he had ever seen the inside of a poolroom before. He looked like an accounting major or some-thing, one of those guys who graduates and disappears into the ano-nymity of a partnership in a CPA firm and lives his life wearing a bored smile.

But this guy came up to me and said, "Mr. Diliberto, are you going to stay in town overnight?" I said I hadn't planned on staying. But he said: "Well, I know I can't beat you, but I'm a student over at the University in Norman and there's people there who like the way

I play and they'll back me if you would like a game of Straight Pool tomorrow. I can promise you seven or eight hundred dollars a game, 150 point games."

This was great! Here I was one of the top Straights players in the world and this kid was offering to basically donate to my wallet for the experience of playing me. I had to go for that. So I said I'd be happy to stick around for such a pleasure and got directions to the Student Union.

The next day I was in action with the students. I got all the side action I wanted off the sweaters on the rail and I had eight hundred on the game. Before you know it I was out ahead of this guy 110-62. I felt comfortable with my safety shot and retired to my chair to start figuring out how much cash this was going to bring me.

That kid got up and ran 88 and out on me. Freaking hit me with a piano. I had another barrel, so I paid everyone and racked them up again. This game he started with a run of 81 balls. He beat me that game too, and I was broke again. This kid later went on to win national titles and play on the pro tour. It was Dick Lane.

All I had to my name was my beautiful Gina Cue. It was a work of art, with hand-laid points and inlays and ivory and stuff all over it. A real show cue. So I asked Dick to loan me three hundred on the cue and said that we would be back in a week to bail the cue out and ready to play some more. So Dick gave up the three hundred and we were back on the highway.

We went to Kentucky, and on up through Pennsylvania doing our road gig. I was scuffling in the poolrooms and Superstroke was teaching higher math to the local teenage store clerks. But a week later we were back in Oklahoma City and ready to complete the promised transaction. I beat Lane the first game and the betting dried up and went away. Those Okies had lots of heart as long as they were winning. When the tide brushed their ankles they got out of the water and the action evaporated. We couldn't even get level. So we got back in the car again and pointed it west.

We had to go in the general direction of Victorville, because that's where Fink and Torra were on holiday and my car was wasting time in the side lot of a garage. At least the weeklong swing through the country had left enough to bail everyone out and soon I was back on the road again, alone with my dogs, cruising along in the ovenware wagon. The dogs and the car ran me out of cash, so the wallet needed refreshing, but at least the family was together at the table again.

Chapter Eleven
THE DEATH OF THE EASY BITE

By the late 60's the bite had turned into the enemy of anyone with an extra dime. The bite 'system' had worked very well for many years, but it had run its course and was withering. At one time, the roadmen were a pretty tight fraternity. When a guy got busted he could ask another player to stake his next effort and the request was honored whenever possible. No one ever lost anything on these 'loans,' because it was like you were standing in a circle and the money that you passed to your left would eventually go around the circle and come back to you from the right when you needed it the most.

But 'bite artists' slashed the money circle apart. They would hit on anyone near them even when they had cash in their pockets, and when it came time for them to contribute to another player's aid they were nowhere to be found. The system failed because many of the participants only wanted in on one end of the transaction. Money that had once been willingly given up, now changed hands grudgingly. People started demanding collateral in the form of cue sticks or cars.

Guys who had been accustomed to dipping in their pockets, became weary of the theft. One generous man who dried up was Rockaway Abe, a sweater who hung out in the Congress Poolroom in Miami. Abe had coffee every day in the coffee shop there and that was where a lot of guys would approach him. Abe was totally deaf in his right ear and couldn't hear anything on that side, so you had to talk to him from the left so that he could hear you.

One day a player that Abe had staked and loaned money to over the years came up to him in the coffee shop and said, "Abe, I need twenty." He was standing by Abe's deaf ear and got absolutely no response, no recognition of his existence. The stick repeated himself: "Abe, I need twenty for this game." Again, no response. Then the guy remembered that Abe was deaf in that ear, so he went over to the other ear and said, "Abe, lend me fifty." Abe looked over at him and said: "Please go back to the other ear."

Wade Crane, who changed his name to Billy Johnson when his given name became so well known that it queered his road action, was so leery of the bite that he took drastic action one year at the Stardust. Wade was one of the great Nine Ball players of the day with a break so large that he garnered the moniker of 'Boom-Boom.'

Around 1970, Wade came to the Stardust event and was just flowing through the tournament chart. On Friday night he was undefeated and liked the looks of the rest of the chart. He figured this was the year that he would win the thing and after dinner he and Cornbread Red decided to relax for a few minutes at the craps table.

They partnered up, threw in twenty bucks apiece, and when the dice got to him, Wade could do no wrong. Holding the dice for one of the longest rolls that the Stardust had ever witnessed, Wade turned the forty bucks into over forty thousand dollars! When his roll ended, Wade and Cornbread cashed out and left the table as winners. When they split up the winnings, each of them pocketed more than twenty-two thousand dollars, more than four times the average yearly income for an American at that time.

Wade knew what would be coming his way next. He had not been a stranger to the bite and had borrowed money from a lot of the guys himself. But it was not those in whom he had endeared a debt that concerned him. It was all the other guys that gave him serious trepidation. Ronnie Allen was there, and Detroit Whitey and a number of others that he knew would bite through his cash like a school of piranha.

Rather than face the sea of outstretched hands that would await him in the tournament room, Wade left the scene. He put some sizable sums of cash in envelopes that he left at the desk for those people he felt deserved a share for their past kindness, packed his bags in the middle of the night, and grabbed a cab for the airport. By the time the sharks were on his trail the next morning, he was home in North Carolina with the phone off the hook.

Cornbread took another tack. He took a slew of his friends shopping the next day and told them he would pay for anything they could lug up to the clerk in fifteen minutes. He spent several thousand dollars buying those in his favor new alligator shoes, sharkskin suits and silk shirts. For the balance of the weekend, he could honestly say that the bite share of his pot was already gone. I walked by the store at the end of the spree and Cornbread still treated me to a pair of alligator shoes.

Cornbread did well by his friends. One of these was his old road buddy, Junior Geoff. Junior Geoff was one of Cornbread Red's best friends and a regular player at both Johnston City and the

Stardust. Junior stood about 5' 3" tall and always wore a nice suit. He looked like an insurance salesman or history teacher. Like Steve Cook, his innocent looks were his greatest hustle. No one could believe that this guy was a shark. After Cornbread finished paying off all the purchases made by the players he took to the store, he sought out Junior and gave him ten thousand dollars.

Junior had driven to the Stardust that year with his wife in their new Cadillac, a black road yacht that made the highway feel as soft as your bed. While we were at the Stardust, his wife got sick and he had to fly her home where she could be with her doctor. So he put her on a plane back to Florida and then came to talk to me.

He said, "Danny, my wife is sick and I've had to put her on a plane home. We both live in Florida, so why don't you ride back with me and we can stop in some spots along the way, have a little fun and make some cash together?" It all sounded pretty good to me so we made our plans to leave the next morning early and cover a lot of desert the first day.

Things were looking pretty good. I had a ride back to Florida in a nice car with the prospect of some good road action and my road partner wouldn't need to hit on me for cash because he had a fresh ten grand bankroll of his own. So Junior and I went to have a late dinner and decide what time to get up for our trip. While we were eating our steaks the public address system paged Junior. "Uh-Oh," said Junior, "That must be Red. He probably went broke and wants his ten grand back. To heck with tomorrow morning, let's leave right now. Forget sleeping, let's just get in the car and get out of here!"

Which is exactly what we did. We left the money for the meal on the table and hit the road right then. We had a pretty uneventful trip. Junior always wanted to make such crazy games that he didn't get much action. The way he would proposition someone was way too complex. It sounded like a snare. "Okay, I tell you what. I'll give you the five-ball and you give me the eight-ball and we can play a set for a few hundred." That sort of deal is hard to go for; you just figure it's too involved to be a straight up deal.

But in New Orleans we went into the Sports Palace and found Ernie Sellers. Ernie was an old road horse who liked to play One Pocket and Nine Ball for pretty decent stakes. When we saw Ernie, Junior told me I should ask him to play, that we had the advantage in that game. Ernie agreed to the game and Junior got busy lining up the side bets. We were only going for twenty a game against Ernie, but there was another two hundred bet over the rail, so we were playing two hundred twenty dollars a game Nine Ball!

We played for hours and hours and when Ernie had had enough and called it quits we counted up our winnings and we were up nearly two grand. Junior and I got back in the Caddy and continued on towards Florida. We got back up on I-10, Junior turned to me and said: "You know, that was business back there. Ernie was dumping for us."

Which was news to me. I said, "Why didn't you tell me that earlier? I wouldn't have dogged it here and there had I known he was on our team."

Junior said, "Well, he was, and we have to send him a third of the money as his cut." His cut was a bit over six hundred and I said, "Well, if that's how it is, then that's just how it is, you gotta do it. Send him the dough."

That settled, we enjoyed the rest of the drive home, I got my cut from Junior, and we parted company. I went back to the Congress poolroom and life continued on as normal. A year later it was time to go back out to L.A. for the Straight Pool tournament and I decided to drive. On the way I stopped at the Sports Palace to see Ernie.

Ernie saw me come in the door and he smiled and came over to me. "Well, Danny, you beat me last year at Nine Ball. How about this time we try some One Pocket?" My first thought was that I needed to avoid this game, since I was not a One Pocket player. It just wasn't my game, Nine Ball was. But what struck me was that the conversation didn't sound right. Something was funny. Ernie wasn't as comfortable with me as he should have been.

So I took Ernie off to one side and asked, "Junior sent you the money we owed, right?" His answer knocked me right out of my socks. "What money? I didn't have anything coming." I told Ernie that I would be back and stormed outside to the pay phone and dropped a dime on Junior.

"Junior, this is Danny."

"Oh, hi Danny! How are ya?"

"Junior, I'm in New Orleans." Silence on the other end. A very long silence. Finally I said: "Junior? Junior? Are you there, Junior?"

Finally he responded: "It's not like it looks, Danny. It's not like it looks." So I said: "Well, tell me how it is, then." More silence. A cold, dead silence. And I said, "Junior, you better get to Western Union and send me my three hundred right now."

He replied, "Danny, I'm short. My wife is still sick and the doctor bills have killed me." I would hear none of it. "Junior, if you want to be friends with me you better get to Western Union and send me that three hundred. I gotta tell you, I'm a little hot right now." When I got to Western Union my money was waiting for me. I never had anything to do with Junior again.

Junior wasn't the only roadman forced into desperate acts. The bad economy at the time affected gamblers as much as anyone. Prices were going up, wages were stagnant, and things got so tough on the road that everyone began to keep an eye on their backs. Even the most revered stakehorses were not immune from the toss.

The 1972 World Series of Poker Champion, Amarillo Slim (real name T.A. Preston), was a tall cowboy who always wore his white ten-gallon Stetson and he played pretty good One Pocket. But his strength was in picking winners and setting up games. It was considered an honor to have Slim stake your game.

A good, honest player can make a decent buck being backed by a horse like Slim. But larceny is always tempting and a lot of players will dump their horse. It's easier than actually striving to win and you know your take before the first ball is struck. All a player has to do is get with his opponent before the match and agree to cut the horse up. Say they're playing for ten thousand. One of them agrees to dump the match and the two players divvy up the cash later. No losers except the horse that got dumped on.

So Slim had been dumped a time or two and he was way too sharp to not realize when he was getting dumped. I walked up next to him one time in Vegas when he was on the low end of a dump and he told me his player had become, "such a low-down son of a bitch that he'd put a rattlesnake in your pocket and then ask you for a match." Money got so tight on the circuit that men who had made a good living in the rooms for years suddenly began to go for long stretches without enough money to cover the basic living expenses like food, clothing, shelter, and the ponies.

No one was immune from the downturn. Steve Mizerak, when Boston Shorty was inducted into the BCA Hall of Fame, got up and told a story about flying into Boston during this period hoping for a score in a town where no one knew his face or name. He got in a cab at the airport and figured the cabbie might be able to steer him to the right room.

He leaned up to the cabbie and said, "Tell me, friend, where does one go in this town for a little friendly pool game? I'm new here and I like to play pool for money. It relaxes me." The cabbie turned around and said, "I'll play ya some, mister." The cabbie drove them to a nice little room a few blocks away and began looking for a house cue. Mizerak felt that he had really lucked into a sucker. Here he hadn't even checked into his hotel room yet and he already had a cab driver on the line willing to play for some handsome money. This, he felt, was going to be a really great trip.

Within eight hours, the cabbie had taken every cent Miz had brought on his trip. His entire stake was gone. Steve didn't even have the money to pay the fare he owed for the cab ride. The cabbie was Boston Shorty and it was he who had gotten lucky that day.

Shorty gave Steve a ride back to the airport au gratis. Miz now had no money for food or a hotel room so he had to go back home and sell some more seafood to raise another stake.

Shorty could really play, and few could top him at setting up a mark. There was a player in Philly at this time named Harry, who was a very good shortstop. Harry always played in the same room, on the same table and if you wanted his cash, you had to go to him.

Shorty was well aware of the advantage that Harry had by playing on the same table every day. That table was home to him, a friendly place to play. He knew every inch of the rails and which pockets were most generous and which were unforgiving. Shorty needed to generate some sort of edge or he could go in there and get his hat handed to him. The plan he came up with was not only original; it was also funny.

Shorty and his backer went into Harry's room, took a seat, ordered a couple of drinks, and sat there quietly and watched him practice. The hook was that Shorty was pretending to be a deaf-mute. He and his backer were going through the charade of speaking with hand signals and Harry would see Shorty occasionally nodding his approval of a good shot or run.

After a while, Shorty's stakehorse got up and went over to Harry and said, "My little friend here would like to play some games with you. He thinks you are a great player and he would get tremendous satisfaction if you would allow him to play a few games with you for some money."

Harry figured there was no harm in accepting a donation from someone wanting to kill a little time and agreed to the game. In those days they played push-out, so there was a lot of motion going on. If Harry pushed out, Shorty would have to motion to him to go ahead and shoot and it was really comical watching Harry come up with hand signals that he thought the deaf man would understand. When he needed to pause to go to the toilet, Harry made a motion that many in the room knew indicated his need in a dramatic fashion. As he passed the rail a woman sitting there remarked, "Darn, I thought you were flirting with me."

The deaf-mute act was great. Harry was totally disarmed and didn't dig down deep enough to grab his 'A' game until Shorty had him far in the hole. Meanwhile, Shorty and his horse were getting a little nervous because it seemed that all the sweaters saw the con and knew that the deaf-mute thing was phony. Harry was a pretty tough guy and the sweaters didn't want to get him upset, so they never let on that they knew that Shorty wasn't mute. It was all straight out of Vaudeville. The whole deaf-mute act was so funny to those in the know, that after a while, whole groups of spectators would go outside and laugh. They couldn't laugh inside or Harry would catch on, so groups of guys would leave the stands, go outside and laugh, and then come back in again. The spectators were constantly rotating in and out.

After only a couple of hours, Shorty was up a couple of thousand, really beating on Harry. He was chasing lost money and seemed embarrassed to be losing to this mute fellow in front of all his friends and admirers. For Shorty, things were going much better than he had expected, so he was relaxed and playing within himself. At a critical point in the match, Shorty slipped up. Harry rolled out to a tough spot. Shorty got up, walked around the table looking at the shot, and then returned to his seat and said, "Ah, go ahead and shoot."

Harry hesitated, confused, but got down and started to shoot. He had the shot all lined up in his sights when it suddenly hit him and he did a double take and jumped up off the shot. "He talked!" screamed Harry, and the entire room burst out in laughter so hard that there were tears flowing. Some were concerned that Harry might tear Shorty asunder, but even he saw the humor in it and paid up. Shorty walked away a winner.

Everyone complained about the degeneration of the road life. Some guys even surrendered to day jobs. The die-hards all hung in there, though. Grady Mathews was overheard complaining about how there was no money in pool and how the sport was no good to anybody and one of the guys listening said: "Well Grady, why don't you just go get a job and quit pool?" Grady looked at the guy like he was a lunatic. "A job? Hell, I can borrow a hundred a day, what do I need a job for?"

But laughs were hard to find. Things got so tight that you had to be constantly on the lookout for rip-offs. And not just from other players. You could get bitten from any direction. Things had begun pretty tough for me in 1968. The highlight of the year came at the BCA Championship in Lansing, Michigan. This was a major, 128-player tournament. Up to this time I had never won a big tourney, but in this one I won the winner's bracket and Joe Balsis, coming from the loser's side in a true double elimination event, would have to beat me two times to win.

THE DEATH OF THE EASY BITE

Willie Mosconi, there as a TV commentator, came up to me, "He has to beat you twice. He can't do it. He can't do it!" I went to bed all excited, thinking I was going to win the biggest tournament in the world. The next evening Balsis beat me twice in front of a national television audience. I never was a good loser, and this one really hurt me bad. I would sometimes have to go hide after a loss so I wouldn't be nasty to people. In this case it was so bad, I went to my room and hid in the bed.

An hour later my phone rang and it was my friend Pete Margo. He was trying to make me feel better and told me I would have lots more chances to win and my future was stretched out ahead of me. He said that he and a bunch of our friends were going out for Italian food and he wanted me to come along and get something to eat.

When the cab picked us up at the hotel I got in front with the cabbie and Pete and two other guys got in the back and started telling each other pool stories while I chatted with the driver. That driver, a hard-working black guy, told me his whole life story about how his mother-in-law lived with them and his wife's sister was a bitch and we got tight.

When we got to the restaurant I asked Fred, the driver, to come on in and eat with us, my treat. I had, after all, just won five grand for second place and in those days you would spread it around when you had it. So he came in and he and I took one side of the table and the other guys sat on the other side, still engrossed in their stories.

Fred the cabbie continued with his autobiography. His daughter ran off with some guy and she was knocked up and messing with drugs and "why can't kids today have any responsibility?" He unloaded a lot of his heart over that meal and I felt pretty good about being the vehicle for his unburdening. We shared a grand meal, drank some wine, had a nice dessert, and when it was done I paid the tab for the table and we went back outside. Fred went to retrieve the cab from the lot and pulled up out front to collect us. When I got in, I saw that the meter read $96.50. He had left the meter running while we ate. Very expensive friendship, the one with Fred the cabbie. One that told of the hardship of the times.

That BCA tournament success queered some good action on the road for me for some months. I was in a room in Georgia playing the local shortstop, who kept looking at me going, "Haven't we met before? I feel like I know you from somewhere." I kept saying that maybe that was so, but that I didn't remember the previous meeting. About four games into our set I looked down on one of the spectator tables and there was my picture on the cover of the magazine the guy had been reading when I walked in! I made an excuse to leave after the first set and retreated to the highway before he could resume his reading.

The times got so tough that the Wade Crane escape became common fare for anyone with cash. The Janscos, in order to avoid the bite themselves, had begun calling the hotel desk and subtracting what you owed the hotel as well as any advances that they had granted before awarding you your prize monies. With them, the further out on the boards your name moved, the higher your credit line became.

One year, this loan policy resulted in my prize fund of almost $1,500 being reduced to the point where when I cashed out, I only got $20. And that, of course, was all the money I had in the world. As I was leaving with my twenty, I heard Jimmy Reid and Jim Rempe talking. They were about to play their match that would determine 5-6th place with the winner continuing and the loser packing it in.

They made an agreement that whoever won the match had to give the loser fifty bucks to go gamble any way the loser wished and they would split any winnings that would result. Well, this sounded pretty neat, so I stuck around and watched their match and Rempe won. Sure enough, he walked right over to Reid and handed him a fifty and they headed out into the casino to pursue fate.

I had to see how their deal evolved so I followed them. Reid walked around and passed the roulette tables, passed the blackjack tables, and finally got the sign from above or whatever he was waiting on and went up to one of the crap tables and stood to the right of the croupier.

He waited for the dice to come around to him. Well, if Reid had a divine vision about how to multiply the fifty, then I wanted to send my twenty along for the ride, so I stood to the right of him. Jimmy started a roll you wouldn't believe. I began betting four dollars to come, four dollars odds, four dollars to come, four dollars odds, and so on. Before the roll was over I was betting five hundred to come and five hundred odds! It went on and on! When the roll was over I was twenty thousand ahead.

"Finally," I thought. "I'm gonna get out of the freaking Stardust with some cash." You must remember, this had never happened before. The Stardust had always been like a tomb for my bankroll. The place was a dark hole where lots of cash went in but none ever came out. So I was standing there with all these black chips in front of me and I was just dumbfounded.

Reid had passed the dice, but he was still in action. Rempe heard his name on the loudspeaker and had to go play his next match, but he was just as happy as a pig in crap. He was rich off of his share of their winnings! So he yelled over to me and good-naturedly asked me to keep an eye on Reid for him and grinned and ran off to play pool. Reid and I were still standing there at the craps table with the dice rattling our ears.

We should have just packed up our chips and headed for the cage and then the airport. The bite on this take was going to be phenomenal. We knew that as soon as any hand holding a cue heard of this, the schemes, formulas and paybacks would be on us like hammers on nails. We would be bit hard!

I came *so* close to leaving. I cashed in my chips and went back and stood by Reid. He just kept playing, figuring it wrong to leave the table while the dice were hot. He was rolling along and the chips were coming into his pile and then leaving again. And every once in a while, he would pick up a black chip and casually drop it into his girlfriend's big, open purse. He was taking out insurance in his squeeze's bag.

We were there for probably another hour and the black chips kept diving into the girlfriend's bag. But many, many more of them were crossing the table and going home again to the croupier's bank. Before Rempe could finish his match and get back to us, all the money had gone back to the casino. Reid had lost it all back except for the insurance money.

THE DEATH OF THE EASY BITE

I still had my twenty grand. Reid and I walked back into the tournament room and Rempe came over to us right in the middle of his match: "How'd it go?" He expected good news. So Reid said, like he's saying it's a nice day or something, "I lost it all." Rempe never said a word. He shook his head a moment and went back to his match.

Instead of heading to the airport like I should have, I stuck around until the end of the tournament. I was figuring that Rempe and Reid wouldn't want it getting around what a fortune they had surrendered, so they may not tell anyone that I cashed big at craps. But the bite was getting really voracious around the room because this was the Stardust and everybody was broke.

Finally I came to my senses and went off to my room to pack and flee. While I was packing, the phone rang and it was Jimmy Reid. "Y'know Danny, you had a pretty good hand down there on me. You really ought to throw me something."

I said: "You want something? Sure, just go to your girlfriend's purse. It's in there." He laughed and hung up and I headed for the airport and home.

I learned something about the bite from Jim Rempe in Tahoe. One time, Jim and I were sitting at the bar having a drink and Louie Roberts came up to him and said, "I have read the entire book on blackjack and I am the expert! I am the greatest blackjack player in the world. Jim, loan me twenty bucks for a starter."

So Rempe looked at him and said: "Louie, I'll let you have the twenty, but you gotta go right over to that roulette table right there and bet the whole twenty on either black or red. If you win you give me my twenty back and go play blackjack. If you lose, you go find another horse."

So Louie took the twenty, bet it on black and won. Rempe got his money back, Louie had his stake, and off he went. Now this was double-smart on Jim's part as he never came off looking cheap by saying no to the bite and yet he had an actual shot at getting his money back, which you never do otherwise.

So Louie went out and gambled the twenty at blackjack and, of course, he lost. He came back into the bar and said: "Jim, let's do it again, let's do it again." And Rempe calmly looked at him and said, "Nope, that's only a one-shot deal. I gave you your chance. Now go find another horse."

Chapter Twelve
THE GREAT GOLF HEISTS

After six years of being in Johnston City every October, everyone had seen all the moves you could make on a pool table. When the Janscos took the land across the road from the Show-Bar and put in a golf course, it opened up a whole new world of possibilities. Many pool players are also good golfers and would gamble on golf courses during the daytime and move into the poolrooms at night.

George and Paulie called their new golf course the Stardust Country Club as a kiss-up to the honchos in Las Vegas who hosted their spring tournaments. The course was an immediate hit with the players who had complained for years that there just wasn't anything to do during your time off of the tables during the tournaments.

It wasn't too long before I found a way to capitalize on the golf thing. I never was interested in the game myself, but I noticed that those who were, developed pretty big egos about how well they could perform with the stick and ball. So I let it be known that I would play clubless against anyone, on the proposition that we would play the short game only and start each hole from one-hundred twenty-five yards out. Most of them assumed it would take me two tosses to reach the green. Plus, I could count on the golfers to assume that their skill with the clubs, so long in the making, would naturally surpass someone just tossing the ball with his hand. I mean, if you could just throw a golf ball, they wouldn't be getting such high prices for those clubs, would they?

Even when the golfers got beat, they couldn't allow themselves to think it was the real deal, so the same guys would keep coming back to donate to me. In the end, everyone finally learned that they had to shoot a two on each hole to win as I was always on the green in one and usually needed only two 'putts' to get out. So I robbed a lot of folks on that deal just because everyone assumed that clubs were an edge, when in fact they were a handicap. Some guys, looking for another 'hook,' tried the proposition about putting with the cue stick, but that just doesn't work. The stick doesn't have the right mass to get a proper roll on the ball. But you can roll a golf ball in with your hand real well.

My original golf bet wasn't on the golf course. That one came about because the Jansco boys were real nut artists who always had other nut artists around squeezing in on the action. George and Paulie were of Hungarian lineage and gave birth to the term 'Hungarian nuts,' a phrase used whenever the bet is an extreme 'lock.' The proposition for them got its inertia one morning at the J&J Ranch, a restaurant near town they owned and where George's wife Sarah made a great breakfast that all the players loved.

One morning, George and Paulie were talking about how far you could throw a golf ball. They believed that no one could throw a golf ball a hundred yards. Both of them played baseball in high school and a little semi-pro ball and they just knew that nobody could throw a golf ball that far. They knew that the local high school heroes couldn't even come close, as they had tried this proposition on them for years and none of them could do much more than throw their arm out.

Ed Kelly was having breakfast at the Ranch when this conversation took place and he called me in my room. "Danny, can you throw a golf ball a hundred yards?" I said, "I dunno." Then he told me the gaff and I said for him to go sit down and act like he had never heard the conversation. I wanted a chance to go out to the local high school football field and try it out. I wanted to have a sure bet and not take a stupid risk.

That afternoon, I got Kelly and a stakehorse named Cuban Joe and we drove out to the high school. We walked out onto the football field and I stood down in one end zone with a couple of Titleists in my fist. I didn't want to throw my arm out doing this, so I was a bit cautious with my first throw. I was just trying to get a feel for what it would take. That first toss sailed right on past the hundred yards and out the other end zone. This thing was really a lock. I never have figured out why my arm is so different from most folks, but I could always throw just about anything. In baseball, my arm was deadly to the plate even when I was backed up to the outfield fence. Cuban Joe saw that this was such a hanger for me that he agreed to take the entire bet for only 20% profit.

That night at the Cue Club, we set it up so that Ed Kelly started the conversation. He set the Jansco boys up by telling them that I was a baseball player who might have enough ego to think I could throw the golf ball. He came up to me with George and Paulie and a couple of their Hungarian friends. He stood next to me at the bar, made a little polite conversation about baseball, and threw the hook.

"Say, Danny, do you think you could throw a golf ball, say, a hundred yards?"

ROAD PLAYER

"Gee, a little golf ball? I used to throw a *baseball* all the way home from center field! And a golf ball isn't nearly as much weight as a baseball!" The money jumped all over me. When the word got around that I was taking this bet, everyone there wanted to wager me down to their pocket lint.

At dawn the next day, we all caravanned out to the same high school football field and everyone showed the dough. We got down for forty-eight hundred bucks and had some pretty sharp cookies on the line. Everyone stood on the sidelines with these big ol' grins on their faces waiting for me to throw that ball. I wound up like a pitcher on the mound and let it fly. Again, it soared from the end zone all the way through the other end zone. When I looked over at the sideline the grins had been replaced by looks of bitter disgust and I got a little bit edgy about making it look so easy. But the Janscos laughed and paid up, so everyone else did as well.

The Janscos weren't ones to lose a bet and just forget about it. I knew they would make an attempt to come back on me. Sure enough, that night at two in the morning, Kelly said they had a guy who wanted to throw baseballs for money. It turned out this guy was a ringer they had called that afternoon and paid to come down expressly to win their money back. He was a pro from the Cardinals. They had him acting like a nothing chump. We smelled the rat and figured that he would be pretty hard to beat, but this just goes back to the old rule that you can't win serious money from a loser. We went right outside and threw the balls and I won again. I had beaten the Hungarian nut artists twice in under twenty-four hours.

164

Eventually, after playing the golf ball bet around the country, I got confident enough that I would take a price on throwing a field goal. Jay Helfert and I were in my hotel room once in Bakersfield. He had gotten in on the tail end of the ovenware action and we were sitting around one Sunday watching a golf tournament and telling stories. We happened to be watching the tube when Jack Nicklaus came up short of the green from 115 yards out.

"Oh, man!" I exclaimed, "I could *throw* a ball that far!" Now, that's the kind of line I always threw out hoping that someone would jump in. I never thought Jay would bite, I was just playing around, but this was an opening Helfert wouldn't miss. To him, this was just an open mouth that had overstepped the bounds of sanity and there was a lesson to be taught here for a small profit.

"No, Danny," he said, "I don't think you can do that. In fact, I'll *bet* you can't do that!" I hesitated long enough for him to think that I was considering backing away from the action, but then I got all swelled up and said if he wanted to lose his money, I was willing to bet all he wanted that I could cover a football field with a toss.

Helfert's eyes lit up like Christmas lights. Here he had an ego on the line and he wasn't about to let go of it. Jay knows that a man's brag quite often exceeds his abilities, so he right away put down a two hundred dollar bet and said he knew of a football field nearby. Before you knew it, we were on the field at Bakersfield High and I was walking out to the center of the end zone. It was a gorgeous day and my arm felt great in the warmth of the California sun.

As I stood there in my end zone, I looked up and saw the goal posts way down at the other end of the field. Jay was halfway down

ROAD PLAYER

to the other end zone when I called him to come back. I walked out
to meet him and he was probably thinking that I wanted to call off
the bet or get better odds or something. Instead, I looked at him real
hard and said, "Can I get a price on throwing a field goal?"

Helfert must have thought he was in a dream. Here he had this
little Italian chump who had already made one ludicrous bet that he
had no way of converting, and now he wanted to make things much
worse for himself! Helfert knew he had to stay calm and not show
any excitement that could scare me off the hook, so he said, "Sure,
you can get a number on that. How about four to one on fifty?" I
shook my head okay and he took off down the field. He was standing right beneath the goal posts and had a friend up with me to make
sure I didn't step over the line. I wound up and threw the ball.

I can still remember Jay's head tilting back further and further
until it was all the way back as the golf ball cleared the uprights. His
head came slowly back down until his eyes met mine. All he could
do was smile and shake his head. He was a nut artist himself, so he
knew he had been set up. But he paid me the four hundred without
so much as a groan.

Like all gamblers, Jay wanted his money back. But he was smart
enough to not hurry the action, to wait for the right moment to make
his move. A few years later, Jay and I and a couple of other guys
drove to a tournament together. We stopped at a rest stop and put
some bottles on a tree stump and played a ring game of hitting the
bottles with rocks. I won every game and had to loan some of the
guys their money back so they could get to the tournament. Jay never
again bet against my arm.

THE GREAT GOLF HEISTS

Titanic Thompson was one of the high rollers who knew I could throw the golf ball. He had heard of the score in Johnston City, so he would put me in action with a golf ball whenever he could. In 1969, I went to Dallas and there was a guy there named JJ who owned a bowling alley and gambled high on bowling and also liked to throw the golf ball. When Ty found out this guy liked to sucker folks on the golf ball bet, he knew it would be easy to sneak me in there.

The only problem I had with this deal was that Titanic was hanging around with George McGann, and just being in the company of this guy was a bit too dangerous for my liking. McGann had a voice that made him sound like Bullwinkle, but he was a stone killer. There were way too many people out there who wanted him dead for me to desire his company. When we were setting up the plan for the golf ball bet in Dallas, we were in their hotel room when the door opened unannounced. McGann and Titanic acted as one and automatically turned over the coffee table and knelt behind it as they drew their guns. The maid walked in, stared down the barrels of their 45's, and asked if we needed any linens. McGann put up his gun and muttered that a diaper might be nice.

Some years later, one of his mortal enemies caught up with him and shot him dead. Whoever did it shot him thirty-five times to make sure he was dead. He was such a bad character, that they didn't ever want to face him again. So they just emptied out on him and reloaded and emptied out on him again and again. You can't blame them for making sure. This guy was so crazy that one time he put his gun on a poolroom owner just because he was asked to not sit on the tables. The man would kill you for a bad look.

But at this time in Dallas, he was still very much alive and getting a share of this deal. The way it was set up, Titanic got me into a bowling match with JJ for chump change which we didn't care about losing. While we were bowling, I picked up the bowling ball and said, "I bet I can throw this farther than you can." And he said, "Well, maybe so, but how do you feel about a golf ball?"

Once again, the best scores are where the condemned tie their own noose. Get someone else to make the bet and you can always take them for a lot more cash. I wasn't there during the payoff, but my end of the deal was worth two grand and I was just happy to be getting out of there and away from McGann.

The golf ball earned me money all over the country, even at home in Miami. Once, a friend had heard of my throwing the ball in Johnston City, and he asked me if I had ever heard of Nick's Lounge, a bar on the intercoastal waterway. When I said that I hadn't, he told me all about this little game they played there.

It seems that the distance across the canal is much greater than it appears. From time to time, the regulars would suck someone into betting that they could toss a golf ball across the water to the other side. No one ever won the bet, including two great arms. Mickey Mantle had failed at his attempt, and so had Roger Maris.

So first, I had to find out how far it really was across that canal. I went over there early one Sunday morning when they were closed and cast a lead weight on a spinning reel across the water. I carefully hauled the line back in until the weight was just on the other shore and then I marked the line. I took the line to my bait shop and had them measure the line for me on the machine they used to sell line by the yard. It measured one-hundred and ten yards.

I knew I could make that throw under the right conditions. But the conditions were rarely right. I needed the wind to be behind my back. The wind blows strong on the Florida coast and can stop a golf ball in mid-flight. The problem was that the prevailing wind, from the east, was always in your face as you stood in the bar.

But I knew it would change at some point. Like when a front would come through. So I had two cohorts on call for this gig and I went to begin laying the foundation for the wager. I dressed in a coat and tie, put on some clear eyeglasses with thick black rims and went to Nick's Lounge every few days for a martini.

I quickly got the reputation as a know-it-all. I would throw in my two cents worth in every conversation, invited or not. I was just an annoying little prick. They had to put up with me, I didn't insult anyone or anything, but I was a pain to be around. They would have loved to stick a scam to me.

After a few months of this, I went in one day and the wind had shifted and was coming across the canal at our backs. The time was right! I called my two cohorts and they came in together maybe twenty minutes later. Soon, the two of them were embroiled in an argument as to whether or not one of them could clear the canal with a golf ball. They made a bet and then the bar joined in. Everyone wanted to bet against the guy who said he could do it.

I wanted to bet, too. But being the know-it-all, I bet that he could do it. I put ten down with one of the regulars. When the bets were all down, my friend wound up and threw that ball as hard as he could. He fell short by twenty-five yards. Everyone settled up and had a good laugh except me. I got hot.

"You lousy bum! You cost me ten bucks because you couldn't throw a lousy little golf ball across that water!" This was the opening everyone in that bar had hoped for. The guy I bet the ten with asked me if I thought I could throw it across. "Sure," I said, "Why not?"

This time the bets came from everywhere and they were bigger. We had one of my cohorts hold all the money, over a thousand bucks, as he was 'neutral' and would pay the winner without a fuss. I walked out to the patio, took off my coat, tie and glasses and heaved the golf ball. As soon as it began to soar one of the barflies screamed, "We've been had!" It was obvious that the golf ball was going to clear the water. It did by several yards. I collected my money and left Nick's Lounge forever.

For a game that I never took up, golf treated me real well. Golfers just refuse to recognize how poorly they play. Billy Incardona took the game up for a while and he used to drive us nuts on the road. Every day, we would have to stop somewhere and let Billy hit a couple buckets of balls. And he was terrible. He was taking lessons and still couldn't get any better. Finally, I told Billy that I had never played in my life and I would give him a stroke a hole for nine holes. We bet dinner with all the trimmings and wine.

I beat him so badly that it was like a heist. I never played golf again. But the really good thing was that neither did Billy.

Chapter Thirteen
JOHNSTON CITY, CLUB WEIRD

Marcel Camp showed up most years at the Cue Club to bet on the matches. Give Marcel some heavy side action and a Heineken and he was good to go. Marcel could sit there and watch match after match and be just as happy as a new dad. He would study every shot of every game and could remember the shots in any given game for days. He lost money betting against me once and came up six months later and asked me why I'd banked a three ball cross-side instead of ducking. I didn't have a clue as to what he was talking about, but he remembered it like it had happened that morning. Marcel Camp lived to gamble and he had developed routines and skills to suit that purpose.

His Achilles heel was that he *had* to have a bet down. One time, Detroit Whitey and Cornbread Red were going to play a set and the word was out that Whitey would be dumping. A new stakehorse had shown up in Johnston City that year and Whitey meant to have the fellow's cash before he ever got sat down good. He got him to back his stick in a game against Cornbread and he was going to dump for half the action. He and Red would divvy up the man's bankroll and send him on down the road.

When I walked in to watch the dump, I saw Marcel sitting there with his little pad out and knew he was figuring what he needed to bet, and on whom, for this match. So I went over and sat next to him and let him in on the news that Whitey was dumping. Then I went off to be with some of my friends. As the match was coming to an end, I overheard someone say: "Wow, that match is gonna cost Camp a buck or two!" I asked about it and he said that Camp had put a wad of money on Whitey. I couldn't believe it. I had told Marcel that Whitey was dumping. I went over to Marcel and he was still sitting there, considering the next match with a smile. "So, Marcel," I said, "I told you that Whitey was dumping and then I heard that you bet on him anyway." He just looked at me and replied, "I had to Danny, I couldn't get any money down on Red."

Marcel was always fun to be around. One time, he made a game to play Nine Ball and wasn't fond of the spot. When they flipped quarters for the break, his coin bounced on the table and jumped right into the corner pocket. He goes, "See, that's how bad I am. I scratch on the flip!" He made some crazy games. In Norfolk, he used to make games with a pencil, shooting with the eraser.

Once at Gulfstream Race Track, I was walking up to the windows to make a bet when I saw Camp coming away from a pay window, counting his money. He had his head down, counting, not paying any notice to me or anyone else around him. A young man ran up from behind and snatched the money out of his hands. The thief was hauling full bore towards me and I clotheslined him and put my foot on his throat. I took the money and gave it back to Marcel. He said "thanks," walked off, and lost it all on the next race.

Johnston City defined the kind of action that Marcel loved. As the years progressed, the action got a lot tougher, because everyone had pretty much established a track record. The first few years, you would find guys from Philadelphia who wanted to back Fusco; guys from L.A. who would put money on Ronnie Allen; while the Detroit group would always bet on Cornbread and so on.

But after these guys matched up with one another a few times, the money got smarter. No one is going to jump up and lay cash on a guy playing straight up against a player who has flailed him the last five times. The spots got so tight; it was hard to make a solid, consistent score anymore. Without big winners in a good mood, the whole money thing falls apart. The more the money moves around in a place, the more chance you have of snagging a piece of it. You can't get to it if it stays trapped in a pocket.

So the action began to slow down among the regional backers in Johnston City as early as 1966. One year, Camp and I walked into the Cue Club together and bumped into Eddie Taylor. Eddie had been there a few days ahead of us to test the waters. When he saw us he just shook his head and said, "No good, guys. Even the *bite* is off 40% this year."

When one pond dries up you must either go to another pond or make one. In Johnston City, the action that was lost on the pool tables shifted over to the golf course or to tossing coins or sports betting. For a while, it seemed like everyone was coming up with a new proposition. Even the broadcasters got into the action. For six years *ABC's Wide World of Sports* came and filmed the tournament at Johnston City and even they got in on the action. Back then it was called "The World Hustler's All-Around Championship." The title was rather ironic since one of the head honchos with ABC, Chet Forte, had a lot of hustle in him.

ROAD PLAYER

He was an all-star basketball player in college, and he came in one day while some guys were putting together a proposition involving basketball and he really snuck up on them. Chet Forte had been around sports all of his life and knew the importance of ego to the success of anyone in athletics. He realized that athletes never reach a zenith until they believe in themselves. Before you can *know* you are the best, you must *believe* that you are the best. In pool, the only sticks with a chance of winning are the ones who believe they will win. No one can win at anything by thinking and feeling like a loser.

Forte crashed into the egos of these guys by letting a group that included Dave Sizemore overhear him tell one of the cameramen that he had beaten a guy one time at free throws and that he had shot his *blindfolded.* When Sizemore heard that, it was like a slap in the face, an insult that anyone thought they were good enough to shoot baskets blindfolded. He turned his head to Forte and said, "You better not give *me* that bet cause I'll shove it down your throat." And Forte says, "Well, come on, big guy, let's see your money." Dave went for his pocket so fast I though he was going to break his thumb.

When word got around about this bet, there were quite a few guys who wanted to watch, so we wound up with another parade of cars going down to the high school. We all went into the gym. Chuck Forte was dressed up nice, like a pro golfer or something, and the rest of us looked perhaps a tad scruffy. We were attired in every poolroom style of the day that you can imagine, which meant anything from Hawaiian shirts to green leisure suits, but all accompanied by alligator shoes. Forte walked down to the coach's office and the alligators parked themselves on the sidelines.

In a minute or two Forte came out, bouncing a basketball with the coach beside him, chatting him up. Forte was to shoot first and walked up to the foul line and squared his feet on the center of the foul line. Sizemore had borrowed a black bandana and tied it around Forte's head and bent down to make sure that he couldn't peek out from under it or anything. When he was satisfied that Forte couldn't possibly see tomorrow coming, he handed him the basketball, stepped back, and said, "Okay, shoot."

Forte popped in foul shots like 1, 2, 3! In no time, he made eight out of ten free throws, took off the blindfold, and looked over to Dave. Sizemore was standing there beside him with a crazed look on his face. He might as well have been out there with his dick in his hand. Dave still had to shoot and he was obviously shaken by events. He walked up to the line and missed his first three shots and it was over. Blindfolded guy 8, Sizemore 0.

Even so, the more the word got around the tournament about this feat, the more guys came up and wanted to try it themselves. There's that good old predictable ego for you. "He might have beaten Sizemore with that crap, but he ain't beating me!" Forte took a couple of more guys on this wager, but then shut it down. He figured that he had made his point and didn't want it to somehow backfire on him on the air.

Forte had seen enough broadcast problems already. In 1967, when *The Wide World of Sports* was filming the goings-on at Johnston City, they let all the players come up and introduce themselves to the camera: "Hi, I'm so and so from wherever," and do a trick shot for the camera. This process was rolling right along when

Martin Kyman, known as Omaha Fats, made his entrance. Martin's trick shot was an impressive one-handed spot shot and we were all sitting there watching him and he just couldn't make it work. He had done this shot hundreds of times; we had all seen it before; but this day he just couldn't make it work. He tried it forty-seven times and it never went.

Chet Forte smiled through all of this and after each new miss he would say, "That's okay, we've got lots of film, let him keep shooting, just let it run out." And Forte was trying to keep Martin focused and calm and get him to relax, to just take it easy and keep trying. It had to go sometime. He finally made the shot and the room erupted in applause as Martin smiled, waved, and put away his cue.

The circus in Johnston City folded its tent for the final time in October of 1972. That was the year that I won the *All-Around Championship* by besting Boston Shorty and Billy Incardona in the final three-man showdown. It was also the year that the Feds raided the place.

The FBI and the IRS claimed later, that they had an informant who told them that Paulie Jansco was the head of a huge bookmaking organization. So one night, we were all minding our own business in the Cue Club when the doors filled up with badges and guns. They lined us all up against a wall like it was a heist and arrested a whole bunch of us and took us downtown and booked us on various gaming charges.

The real pain was that they confiscated everybody's money, so we were all broke and had to pay lawyers most of our money just to get it back. Only Jim Rempe escaped the robbery. He had won seven grand playing Nine Ball and had taken the cash out and locked it in the trunk of his car. It was still waiting on him when he was released the next morning and he drove away with it. The rest of us had to go through the lawyers and a ton of paperwork.

The trials, those that occurred, were a joke. Most charges were dismissed before ever seeing a courtroom when the Feds realized how bogus their case was. When the Judge put Minnesota Fats on the stand it became the comedy hour. He told the judge, "You should be ashamed! You got that player over there for bringing a ham sandwich across state lines. You got this guy for having a concealed hot dog." And he went on from there with a monologue that even the bench found humorous. Eventually, they dropped all the charges against everyone, but it killed the event forever.

The man who had dominated Johnston City was Wimpy—Luther Lassiter. The best that any one player ever did in Johnston City, outside of Wimpy, were several guys who won two or three individual or All-Around titles. Wimpy won fifteen of them! That's how serious he was. It didn't matter who was playing him what, except maybe Eddie Taylor at One Pocket, Wimpy was the favored side of the betting line. He just played too good to bet against. People tried all kinds of betting lines on him and he wound up beating them all.

Lassiter stood around 5' 10" with gray hair and weighed about 165 pounds. He spoke with a slow southern accent that could disarm you with its calm. And Wimpy was a nice man. He treated everyone well and always over-tipped waitresses. Everyone who knew him liked him. People would try to get him to partner up and go out on road trips, but Luther would say, "Naw, I got to get back to North Carolina. It's time to walk in the woods and look at the squirrels again." And he was just that way. He couldn't wait to get home. When he wanted action, he would just shoot up the road a ways to Norfolk and find another sailor.

Luther had his strangeness. Sometimes he would go on a binge and stay drunk for two weeks. Other times, he wouldn't have a drink for months. He really was pretty much of a lone wolf and stayed to himself. Supposedly, he had a real tragic romance one time, where this woman just broke his heart. He fell in love with a local girl and they got engaged. He loved her to death, but he was the only guy in town who didn't know she was banging every hammer in town. He had already bought the furniture for their new apartment when a friend finally clued him in. He was devastated and I always thought that cost him his trust of people.

I always thought Luther was a hypochondriac, but he finally died and won that bet. He would come to the tournaments and when you went in his room, there would be pill bottles everywhere. There'd be ten bottles on the dresser, nine bottles on the back of the john, and more in his bag. He would take huge handfuls of vitamins several times a day.

I first met him in 1963 and he asked me how my health was. At the time it wasn't actually all that great. I told him I had a few problems here and there; that my stomach gave me a lot of trouble, and he looked up and he said, "Good, then you'll be a great player."

A promoter came up to Wimpy once in Johnston City. He had set up a deal for Wimpy to travel around and do a series of sixty exhibitions. Luther would get $1,000 for each one. That was really big money, $60,000 for six months work in the sixties when a hamburger was fifteen cents. Lassiter politely thanked the man and declined. "Naw, it's time to go home for a while."

He really had no need to hustle on the road. All the action came to him since every hot shot knew that the road to the top led through him. People would wait around Norfolk for him and they would try him at Nine Ball. He loaned most of them bus fare to get home.

Even with all of his greatness, he aged into a sad, somewhat lonely character. In one of the Straight Pool Championships in L.A., the players would gather each evening in the hotel bar. One evening, a player named Danny was talking up this gorgeous hooker in there. The beauty and class of some of the call girls in hotels throughout the world has often surprised me—you might think the profession would draw nothing but trash, but some of these girls, you'd be proud to have on your arm anywhere. This was one of those girls.

She was adorable and had a body that demanded attention— ripe all over with a tiny little waist that looked like you could wrap your hands around it and still twiddle your thumbs. Her face looked like it jumped off of a magazine cover. Everyone in the room was blatantly staring at her as she sat there talking a deal with Danny. Luther was there and he was just overcome with her. He was sitting in his chair and, I swear, his mouth was agape.

This guy Danny was a friend of Lassiter's and felt sorry for him, I guess, because of Luther's betrayal by that girl back home and all.

Anyway, in his own weird way he tried to take care of Lassiter, so he included him in his deal with the hooker.

He was asking this hooker about price and she said she could offer herself that evening for a certain price that she named and Danny accepted. Then Danny asked, "Well how much more if my friend over there gets to watch?" and he nodded his head toward Luther. And she said, "Oh, another fifteen bucks." So Danny said, "Okay, let's go." He went over and grabbed Luther by the arm and the three of them headed to the elevator and Luther's eyes grew wider the longer that Danny leaned into his ear.

Well, the whole bar knew what was going on. The entire negotiation had unfolded with an audience. So a group of us decided that the only thing to do was to climb up the fire escape and watch the entertainment. So a whole slew of us went outside and jumped up and pulled the ladder for the fire escape down, and up we went; up eight flights of outdoor iron fire escape.

We all knew which room they were in, so up we went and sat outside the window in a tight little cluster of voyeurism. We couldn't see all the way into the room because of the way the blinds were set, so nobody really knew what was happening inside the room. All we could see was Luther sitting in the corner watching. So that's what we did, we sat on the fire escape and watched Luther watch.

Finally one of us lost it and laughed too loud. Then it was all hands hell bent for leather, down the fire escape as Danny threw glasses at us out of the window. Luther never got out of his chair. He just sat there and let his eyes wash his heart with that girl's body.

Chapter Fourteen
THE FALL RUN

Fall is a great time of year to start a road trip. The heat that beats you up so badly in the summer is gone and the days begin to shorten so the poolrooms fill up earlier. But in the fall of 1971, I wasn't planning on going anywhere. I was comfortably ensconced in the Congress poolroom in Miami and had enough action going to maintain my dog and horse betting with enough left over that I could cover any game that strolled in without needing to hunt a stake.

One day an old friend, Dick Hall, came into the room, bought a couple of beers, and sat down beside me. Dick and I had run around some together, kicked around in some poolrooms, and made a few bucks. Dick, always in action, was never out of money. He was from Kentucky and had lived near Lexington for a number of years. Dick had played basketball at the University of Kentucky and had become such good friends with Pat Riley that he was best man at Riley's wedding.

He took a pull from his longneck and after he enjoyed the cool swallow he turned to me. "Ya' know the tobacco crop is coming in soon in Kentucky. When it does, everybody has a ton of money. Cash floats around everywhere and the action gets to be pretty darn good. We should make a trip."

I had absolutely no reason to get up and take another trip, but turning down an old friend was never in the equation. "Gimme a minute, Dick."

I kept a big road bag in my room and could toss everything I owned in there in just a matter of minutes. I checked out of my room and went over to the Congress and waved Dick outside. He slugged down the rest of his beer and we had Miami behind us in less than an hour after he first posed the question.

One of our first stops was a place we had heard about for years and never frequented. It was in the foothills of North Carolina in a room owned by a man known to the world as 'Mountain,' one of the most memorable characters I've ever met. He had a skull that must have been three times thicker than normal, because nothing that hit his head could hurt him.

Mountain had a standing wager that he would butt heads with anyone for any amount of money they cared to wager. A pro football lineman showed up once to challenge him on this bet. Mountain spotted the guy a *helmet*. The two of them backed up a few yards, charged, and crashed into one another at full speed. The lineman with his crushed helmet was taken to the hospital unconscious and the doctors feared the onset of coma. Mountain collected his winnings from the lineman's buddy and went back inside to work without so much as a headache.

Once when he was playing Buddy Hall, Buddy got concerned due to Mountain's habit of talking to his cue stick. When he would miss a shot, Mountain would sit down and give his cue a tongue-lashing. When he lost a third consecutive set, he snapped his cue over his head and went to the wall and fetched another one. After Buddy cleaned out his bankroll, Mountain ran across the room, launched himself into the air and collided head-first with the cigarette machine. The machine crushed in like a cardboard box.

Mountain wasn't the only player I'd seen who would beat himself up. There was a guy we knew as Tony the Weasel who would punch himself. I was in his hotel room once after he had put on a really poor performance. He just walked up to the mirror, cussed the image there, and punched himself right in the chin. After his eyes cleared he saw himself in the mirror and said, "Still standing, huh?" and hit himself even harder. That blow took him to the floor.

Mountain began his act as soon as we came in. He would miss a shot and bang his head on the rail so hard it hurt to watch. When we beat him so badly that he had to quit, he started putting the balls back in the egg crate to return them to the counter. He called out to us and we turned around as he threw the balls high into the air. He just stood there and the balls rained down on his head and then bounced off and ran across the floor. I've never seen anything like it. For years I never told anyone about it. I figured no one would believe me. But now, there are enough folks out there who saw this guy do his thing that I have plenty of back-up. We left there richer and eager to get to Kentucky.

Kentucky is a different kind of place. We made it through our first few towns unscathed. Bowling Green was uneventful, as were Beria and Richmond. Nice, friendly action with the farmers. No need to hustle anybody, just go in and announce that you're the best player in the room and you're ready to back up the brag, and the country boys would line up to knock you out of your hayloft.

And some of them could. Kentucky is pool-playing country. Folks around parts of Kentucky raise their kids with a shotgun in one hand and a cue in the other. So if a pair of Kentucky overalls gets you engaged in a set of Bank Pool or One Pocket you could be sponsoring the new tractor.

Usually it went the other way and we would take a couple of hundred off each guy in line and then buy 'em each a beer and put some money in the jukebox and everybody parted friends. But some of these boys descended from that strain of Kentuckian that once considered slaughtering Indians just a part of clearing the land. Playing these boys was like juggling nitro-glycerin and you really didn't want to be around when they went off. You never knew you were in a dangerous situation until the fuse was already lit, and then job one became getting out of there and back on the road while suffering as little harm as possible in the process.

One of these situations arose in Winchester. I should have known better than to go up against the locals in a town named after a gun, but that's all hindsight now. In Winchester, we ran into Mitch. Mitch was a stout six-footer and he agreed to play Nine Ball and I was robbing him. Every time he handed over the cash, he would ask to change to Bank Pool and I would always decline. "No, you know I'm from Buffalo via Miami and you just don't play off the cushions in those parts of the country."

Finally I had dug such a hole in Mitch's pocket that he said he couldn't go on with it. He felt that since he agreed to play Nine Ball with me, then I should agree to play Bank Pool with him. Dick called me over and said, "Look, you're beating this guy so bad, I don't think Bank Pool's going to help him. I think you can take him at anything he wants to do."

So, what can you do? I told him we could play some Banks. We were playing a race to three for a couple of hundred. Sure enough, I beat him the first set without really breaking a sweat. He kept getting out of line like he was nervous or something. He picked it up a bit in the next round and took me to double-hill for the set. In fact, it went down to where we both only needed one ball and I needed to bank the six cross-sides to win.

By now, Mitch had begun the transformation from nice guy to imposing menace. He had grown angrier now that we were beating him at his own game and he was beginning to regret the grand or so we had already accepted from him. I was on the case six-ball and if I sank it, that would be the demise of his last barrel. But not being a Bank Pool player, I didn't exactly hit this thing with that smooth Eddie Taylor stroke. Instead, I trickled it rather timidly across the table and it came up close to just hanging there. But as Mitch rose from his chair, it leaned a little and finally succumbed to gravity and tumbled in.

As soon as that six-ball plopped, I saw the rapid movement out of the corner of my eye. I ducked, and Mitch's cue came down across the table like an axe and shattered as if it were explosive. He had hit the table so hard, the impact sounded like a 12 gauge going off next to my ear. There was no doubt of his intent on that cue. He wanted it to suffer and die.

From my new post under the table, I waited for the cue fragments to finish ricocheting to the floor before I peeked out and met

Mitch's eyes. I was in a bit of a fix, as I was six feet away from his chin and needed to reach it to knock him out and escape. But he looked down and said, "Oh, I'm not mad at you. I'm just mad at me!" We took the money and left with a new appreciation for the emotional content of tobacco farmers.

After the escape from Winchester, we hit a few more Kentucky spots to increase our expenses fund and then headed over to Nashville. Things began real well there. The first room I walked into, one of the locals came over and asked if I wanted to play a few sets. That's a great sign because then I couldn't be cast into the role of the hustler. No matter what happened, I'm not the one who started it. All I did was accept an invitation to play and that makes for much more passive scores.

This guy was trying to hustle me and he only had two paths to follow. He could try to jump out to an early lead and try to make me chase lost money, or he could have me win the first few sets to build up my confidence. Either road takes me where I want to go, an opportunity to raise the stakes and involve the birds on the rail. And that put me in position to make a good score.

I wanted this guy to be good and to think he had the nuts. Over the years I have won a lot more money from players who actually had a shot at winning, than from those who didn't have a prayer. I wanted his greed to come to a healthy boil. Whenever I played some guy who said, "I don't want to take your money," I got out of the game as fast as I could. If the guy isn't greedy enough to accept an easy robbery, then he won't go off himself.

But when this fellow and I started playing Nine Ball, I saw right away that we were going to have to adjust the game, because he couldn't swim in my waters. He might make three or four balls, but he rarely threatened an entire rack. As soon as he asked for the eight, I gave it up. He still couldn't drop a money ball and he asked for the seven and got that as well.

Things were now turning tense. I had won seven hundred before he changed the game the first time and now he was about to ask for the six ball and it was real obvious that he had become the prey of his own hunt. The sweaters were starting to grumble. When you start to hear, "Who is this guy?" from the sidelines, it's time to consider scheduling a retreat.

The room continued to simmer as I gave up first the six, and then the five-ball behind it. The crowd had reached a consensus that this guy was never going to outstroke me and that I probably knew that after the first game. I was starting to rely on Dick's physical presence. He wore thick glasses, but he was a burly guy who obviously didn't take any gruff off of anyone. He was answering the challenges of the sweaters and reminding them that no arms were twisted here and that they could have pulled up anytime they wanted.

Just as I was ready to take the next rack apart, Dick walked up to me with his hand up. He wanted to say something before I broke. "Hey, Danny, I don't want to get you nervous or anything, but there's a guy back here with a gun, and he says if you run another rack he's going to shoot you. He means it."

"Alright, Dick, I tell you what. I'll keep everyone's attention in here while you get out the door, get the car running and pull up with the passenger door open so I can leap in and we can get the hell out of Dodge."

Dick made his way to the door and I started stroking for the break shot, but pulled up and rubbed the shaft like it was sticky or something. I laid the cue down on the table and ordered a round of drinks for the crowd and excused myself to the bathroom. "I have to wash my hands, they're sticky." Halfway across the room, I turned left and was out the door like a shot. Dick's timing was perfect. I never had to break stride to get into the passenger side and we were a block away before anyone moved. We had to leave the last bets on the table, but we were up five grand so we just considered that the insurance payment and went to another spot across town.

What we really needed now, was not another score but some reliable local information. Each guy you play on the road has information that you need in the form of two or three more guys he has played and whose speed he knows. Their knowledge is what keeps your client list growing. We knew that Nashville could now become dangerous for us, so we needed information about other towns down the road. The very next place we went into, I managed to lose ten bucks to a guy and that gave me just enough time to hear about some action going down in Bainbridge, Georgia. Bainbridge was on route 91, which was not a big highway, but at least it was pointed south, towards home in Florida.

The action in Bainbridge was in a black poolroom. Racism had split the populace into two groups, racists and the rest of us. The bigots were in the minority and the civil rights act had passed seven years earlier because so many of the rednecks couldn't read a ballot. Bigots wouldn't have anything to do with blacks, so when we walked into a black poolroom it was cool, as the patrons knew that no bigot would do that. They welcomed us in and the first one who spoke to us was a fellow in a straw hat who asked, "Can a nigger buy you boys a beer?" Dick replied, "No sir, but *you* can."

After the beers were opened and a toast to health was made I said, "We're looking for Shake N' Bake. We understand he might honor a request to gamble at pool." The straw hat considered us for a moment and then said, "Indeed he will, but you better be good if you're gonna play him. He don't lose much."

We had been there about half an hour when Shake (Edgar White) walked into the room. This match was a true relief after the one with the Tennessee rednecks. We took just over a grand from Edgar and his friends before they pulled up. When we bought the house a round, Edgar came over, shook our hands, and said, "There's a spot across town that calls me when someone comes in looking for a game. I'll just make myself unavailable and you can go make a harvest."

He gave us directions to the Rialto Poolroom. Man, this place looked promising! There were four nine-foot tables in there and a big sports board on the wall with all the lines for baseball and football. If there was an action spot in Georgia, this was it. The Sheriff's car leaving the parking lot indicated that the action, if not sanctioned, was at least tolerated.

The bartender was a mountain of a man. He stood about 6'7" and featured three hundred pounds of 'don't mess with me.' I smiled and asked him if there was any Nine Ball action around. He said, "Well, Greg plays, but I don't see him around. He hasn't been here today." So I handed him a ten-spot and asked him to make the call for me. He went to the phone, dialed the number without looking for it, and came back over and told us Greg was on his way.

When Greg came in, it occurred to Dick that he must be the barkeep's brother or cousin or something, because he's another solid guy, but blonde and full of smiles. Looks like another friendly game.

He goes, "Hi guys, I got the call. What do you want to do?"

"I play Nine Ball."

"Ok, let's go. Twenty a game Nine Ball."

Dick loaded up on side action and by the time we were ready to start, he had about ten times the side action that I had on the table. Counting the side action, I was playing Nine Ball for more than two hundred a game with a house cue. In those days you would never walk into a room with a custom cue. You walk in with your own weapon and they would ask for weight right off. On the other hand, sometimes you can find a good house cue and sometimes you can't and if you're shooting with a club, you're giving weight anyway.

I lost the flip and Greg broke the balls and it sounded like a shotgun. You can tell a lot about a guy by his break shot. Ball-bangers just load up and whomp the rack but a real player hits them strong and still controls the cue ball. Greg made a couple of balls and the cue ball squatted right in the center of the table. As he was running the rack, he stopped about halfway through and had words with a young man watching the game. Things escalated between the two and suddenly he threw his cue down and they were going at it tooth

THE FALL RUN

and nail. These boys were at war. They were rolling around on the floor landing punches that sounded like home runs and choking and really trying to do each other grave harm. They weren't trying to bust open the other fellow's lip, they were trying to bust open heads!

Dick walked up beside me and his eyes looked like he had just lost his favorite puppy. "Man, look at this. We finally get some decent action and our mark is either going to die or go to jail." The battle continued around the floor of the poolroom until eventually the fellow Greg was bashing gave up and Greg rose, standing over him.

Some bystanders helped the battered loser to his feet and led him limping out the door. Greg walked over to us. "Guys, I'm real sorry about that. I'm going to play some more and all, but let me calm down a second. I'll go sit down over there for a minute."

Now maybe that should have been a sign to us. Maybe we should have seen the red flag. But like Dick says, this was the first decent action in a while. You can't walk away from the dinner table before they even serve the salad.

Still huffing a bit, Greg managed to finish out the table to win the first game. He turned out to be a pretty good Nine Baller and after an hour of back and forth play, Dick and I were stuck three or four games. Dick came up to me and said, "Let me get the cue." In the car I had my Balabushka, a stick with which I was very comfortable. But I resisted, afraid it might queer the action.

But as the hours went by it got worse and worse and finally we were down to our last few barrels and Dick came up for the ninth time and said, "Let me get the cue." I finally capitulated. Dick got the Balabushka and screwed it together and laid it against the wall near the table. Then he went back and resumed the bets with about twenty guys sitting around him, telling him what a friendly place this was and how you never had to worry about the money here and stuff like that. They were all big winners and real friendly.

With the Bushka in my hands again, things began to click and in the next few hours I won all our money back and about three grand of theirs. Dick was buying everybody beers and telling jokes and trying the best he could to keep the party going. But the boys just weren't as happy now as they had been when they were winning.

About that time, this tush-hog who had been sitting quietly in the corner the whole time and had not placed one single bet on the games, came plodding over to me and growled: "Gimme five hundred."

Now I had already tipped the Tarzan behind the bar sixty bucks and bought the house yet another round of drinks. I wasn't feeling a tremendous need to exhibit much more generosity, so I said "No." This guy was obviously bent on trouble, so I quickly added, "I can't give it to you anyways; it ain't my money. My partner has a say in the money. I gotta go talk to him." By now the guy was holding me by the shirt and I was trying to figure out if he really wanted the money or would just prefer to squash my skull down inside my neck. But he released the shirt and sort of grunted me along.

Dick was against the far wall next to the bar and I went up and told him about the funding request. The beast stayed right on my heels as I crossed the room. When I got up to Dick, I said: "Dick, this guy wants five hundred."

Dick asked, "For what?" and I said, "Because he wants it." And the great white ape nodded in intimidating agreement.

So Dick talked to me like this guy wasn't hanging on my shoulder, and said, "Well, he ain't gonna get it!"

So I turned around and said to the ape, "Well, you ain't gonna get it." The beast went into a big, silent scowl and grabbed me with his left and cocked back a big right-hander and as he delivered, I ducked. The punch landed square on Dick's jaw and his mouth volcanoed blood and suddenly it looked very ugly in Georgia.

When that punch landed, it woke up everybody in the place and they all grabbed the big guy and separated him from us. They were yelling at him, calling him the Carpetman. "C'mon Carpetman, relax!" But Carpetman was in no mood to calm down. He struggled against his captors and the whole time he screamed, "I'm gonna kill ya if I don't get that five hundred! Gimme my five hundred!"

I looked back over at Dick and he was dabbing the blood with his handkerchief and he was pissed. Dick wasn't the kind of guy to just take a punch and walk away. He wanted revenge and he wanted it right now. But I just wanted to survive the trip to the car. "Dick, there's twenty of 'em. Let's just get to the car with the money!."

By now the herd had dragged the Carpetman to the other side of the room, still screaming, but at least now he was some sixty feet away. He continued with his screams: "I'm gonna get my five hundred. I'm gonna get it in here or I'm gonna get it outside and I'm gonna get it today or I'm gonna get it tomorrow, but I'm gonna get MY FIVE HUNDRED!"

Something in me just snapped. I was no longer even considering the consequences of my actions. Reason had given way. I had been holding back Dick, but then my own mouth got fired up. "Y'know

I'm trying to give you the benefit of the doubt," I said, "I'm really trying to figure out why you got five hundred coming." And I'm slowly moving in Carpetman's direction and the noose of arms around him is starting to loosen. "I'm trying to give you the best of it to give you this five hundred, but, y'know what? There's no reason on earth that I'm supposed to give you five hundred and you ain't gonna get it! Turn him loose!"

And I'll be damned if they didn't turn him loose. He came running across the room and I planted my feet and wham! I hit him a shot in the jaw with everything I had. He went rolling across the floor and I knew I had done some damage. The whole crowd now turned on us and they soon had us down, beating us and even biting so hard that I had marks for days later.

Dick was trying to get through the rolling melee to get to the Balabushka so he could bash some heads with it. With one hand I was warding off blows and bites and with the other hand I was trying to hold the Bushka under the table out of Dick's reach and things were looking a little dim.

But remember Tarzan, the bartender I had tipped sixty bucks? He came out from behind the bar and waltzed into the middle of the brawl just throwing people off, first to one side and then to the other, as he cleared his way to the middle where Dick and I were being murdered. He threw hillbillies around like they were rag dolls. And as he came in he was growling loud: "These guys didn't do nothing wrong and ain't nobody gonna bother 'em in my bar!"

He got to us and picked us up and took us behind the bar. There he opened an old door in the wall and it led into a little storage room and at the back of the storage room was another door that led outside. This door was shut with boards and nails. He pried the boards off with his hands and let us out. We made our way around to the car and got in.

Just as we got the car started, we looked up and here came Greg, the originator of all circumstances Georgian. He was running towards the car and we didn't know what might be on his mind. But he was running faster than we could back out and when he reached my window, which of course was open, he said: "Guys, I'm sorry that happened. I enjoyed playing with ya and I'm sorry 'bout the problem in there."

Highway 91 South looked like the yellow brick road. Still, neither of us relaxed until we made the turn onto the highway and knew they probably could no longer find us. The two-lane would eventually lead us to I-75 and that would take us home to Miami. Dick busied himself driving and was silent for hours, never saying a word. Occasionally, he glanced in the rear view mirror and dabbed his mouth, but not a word was uttered.

Finally, well inside the Florida line, he looked over at me, "Danny, you told me that there's too many of 'em, that we gotta just get out of there, and then *you* hit him. I shoulda been the one to hit him!" He went back to driving then and never said anything else. It was satisfied silence all the way to Miami. After all, this time we weren't going back to the barn without our saddle.

Chapter Fifteen
THE NAKED HEIST

After television reduced the attention that they gave to the game, the future of the tournament player dimmed rapidly. Without the money from sponsors that the television exposure brought, the prize funds gradually shrank to where you had to win to survive. A player's income now had to come from the road or from a job and nothing spoils a great stroke like work.

Some of the road schemes were clever and some were dangerous. Even the straight-up man-on-man games could yield unexpected results. Greg Sullivan, who now owns Diamond Billiard Products and produces the annual Derby City Classic All-Around Tournament in Louisville every year, was once a player who wouldn't back away from a challenge.

The way I heard the story, he was playing a fellow in Kentucky one night and wound up quite a bit ahead. He was a seventy-five hundred winner when the poolroom closed at 2 AM. So Greg unscrewed his stick and he and his road partner went over to get paid.

"I don't have that kind of cash on me, fellows. I can give you a check or I can go to my bank when it opens and get you the cash." Greg and his buddy had seen worthless paper before, so the check was out of the question. Greg told him they would go to the bank together and that they would be staying together until the bank opened.

"Fine" said the loser. "Come on over to my place and I'll fix you some breakfast and we can shoot the breeze 'til the bank opens."

That's just what they did. They went to this guy's house and sat in his kitchen and ate scrambled eggs and toast and bacon and when the bank opened a few hours later, they all piled in Greg's car and headed off to get paid.

Taking directions from their hostage, Greg found the bank and parked out front while his loser went in for the cash. They had been sitting in the car for only a few moments when Greg got nervous. He told his buddy, "He could have just gone in the front door and out the back. I'm going in to see what he's doing or if he's even in there."

When Greg walked into the lobby, there was his man, filling out a withdrawal slip at the counter, which he took over and handed to one of the tellers. Greg could see the teller look at the slip, then open her drawer and begin retrieving money. So he knew everything was kosher and walked right back out to the car and sat down. "Sure enough, he's in there getting our money. He'll be right out."

A moment later, out came the man with their money. He walked up to the open window on the passenger side and threw a canvas bank deposit bag full of cash onto the front seat beside Greg. "Here's the money I owe you. Nice knowing you, see you later." And he walked off through the parking lot to the backside of the shopping center. Greg and his road buddy were sitting there grinning at the bank bag when the dye bomb went off and the bank alarms sounded.

Now, Greg and his friend were sitting in their red-interior Chrysler wearing matching pants, shirts, shoes and skin. When the red dust cleared, they knew that they were had. They looked like red ghosts; everything was red except their eyes. So they got out of the car and sat on the front steps of the bank and waited for the authorities.

The FBI questioned them separately for over four hours and, since they were both telling exactly the same story, they let them go after getting the robber's name, address and description. When the cops arrested the guy, he corroborated what they said, and they were completely out of harm's way.

There's a player out of Dallas named Al, and the following ploy was attributed to him, though I have heard of several teams that have used this same approach. Al was talking to another player one time and was told that there was some action going down in Jackson, Mississippi, and he was all used up there. Maybe Al ought to go and check it out.

Al went to Jackson and surveyed the scene and that night, devised a plan to move some of the local money into his account. He called his old friend Lee and laid it out. Here's how it worked, a scheme sometimes called "The Strangers."

Al went into the poolroom the next day and announced that he was the best player in Jackson and in Mississippi for that matter. He challenged any stick in the room to gamble and offered to let them 'make a call' if they needed to rustle up the right kind of action. Al, one by one, went through every player they could set up against him.

They kept trying him and every day the pattern was the same. Some player would get his nerve up or get the spot he thought he needed to win, and Al would strip his wallet bare. He got all the cash that the small fries had and forced them to pull up. The big money wouldn't go up against Al—they could see his stroke was too pure and his moves were too slick to be able to have a fighting chance of winning. They all agreed that Al could sure play pool and after five days, Al had no one to play.

So he spent the next day buying everyone drinks and swapping jokes and stories and at the end of the day everybody liked Al a bunch. Al was a great guy and friend and one heck of a pool player as well. That night, Al went back to his room and called Lee.

The next afternoon began as a repeat of the day before. Al and his new buddies were sitting around a table laughing at each other's stories when in walked Lee. He walked over to the wall, grabbed a stick off the rack, got a crate of balls from the counter, and commenced to knock the balls around by himself. Well, he wasn't holding anything back and he was clearing the table time and again without ever missing.

One of the locals began to notice his game and pointed it out to Al. "Al, look at this guy shoot. He hits 'em pretty sporty." Al looked over there for a minute and said: "Yeah, sure enough, he shoots a nice stick." A few minutes go by and one of the larger moneyed guys, who had refrained from betting against Al, asked: "Al, can you take him? Do you think we could get up a game with him and make some money?" Al assured him that if the stranger would play, he could beat him and there was really no doubt as to that.

Everyone had seen how Al played. They thought of him as the cue that couldn't be beat. So they told Al to try and set up a game and take the guy down. Al had an even better idea. "I'll go play him and I'll lose the first few games until we can get the bet up to a decent level. Then we can sink the hook and clean him out. We don't want to scare him off after the first few racks."

This required a little more investment to set up, but the rewards sure seemed worth it. So Al got the stranger he had known all his life to play for twenty a game. After he lost four out of six of these, he complained that the bet wasn't high enough to keep him focused, so they raised it to fifty a game.

Al also came out the narrow loser on this bet and soon began to jawbone the stranger into something 'worth playing for.' The stranger 'bit' and suggested a race to eight ahead for ten thousand and pulled a wad of bills from his pocket to back up the challenge. Al walked away from the table and back over to the rail and winked and grinned at his new 'partners.' "Put your money up, boys, its payday." And the consortium there of ten to fifteen guys soon matched the bankroll and after a delay to figure out who would win how much according to their original investment, the match was on.

Al surged out to five ahead in the race to eight ahead in about an hour. The cocky stranger taunted the rail and asked if anybody wanted to 'press' the bet. He got another twenty-five hundred in action off the rail, making it a twelve thousand five hundred dollar set. Al had a bank shot on the eight ball to get out on the nine, the kind of shot he had hammered all week, and he missed it! The spectators later said that's when they saw the change. For the first time, it appeared that Al looked a bit unsure, maybe even nervous.

Slowly the newcomer whittled away Al's edge, and then went up by three games. Beads of sweat were suddenly appearing on lips throughout the room. Within an hour, Al was unscrewing his cue, shaking his head, and the stranger was walking out with the money. Everybody tried to console Al, saying he had tried his best but he just wasn't getting the rolls you have to have to win, and not to sweat it. And Al said, "Yeah, I guess so." And left for his room.

The next morning when one of Al's new buddies called his room, he was told that Al had checked out the night before. In fact, by then Al was back in Texas, and he and Lee had already split the pot and headed for other pastures.

Sometimes, trips just turn out sour. Bob Ogburn called me early one morning from South Carolina. "Are you on call?"

"For you," I said, "I'm always on call."

And just like that another trip began. "Make reservations to fly into Greenville-Spartanburg tomorrow. I'll call you back in half an hour to find out what time I need to pick you up."

The next afternoon I was in Bob's car heading for the Holiday Inn and listening to the blueprint. He was still talking when we walked into his room and there was a stack of a thousand ones on the coffee table with the bank wrapper still around them. "What's this?" I asked.

"Oh, I've been here for a few days and I've made some good money, but I can't spend the dough here because it came from a bank job." Well, that pre-qualifies the mark. Anyone greedy enough to stick up a bank is greedy enough to go off big time. But there are those out there who might say this should have been a tip-off. Maybe, some would say, I should have got back on the plane to Miami. It's not like there's nothing to do in Miami. In Miami, action comes and goes with each new wave of tourists.

But the lure of stacks of money demanded that I listen to the deal. That night we went to check out the poolroom. We went into an office building and down a long hall to get to the poolroom in the back. It was just a little four-table room. While we were there, we ran into Eddie Burton's horse and set up a game for the next day.

Bob had actually already set this deal up and we only finalized it that night. I would play Eddie a set of One Pocket and a set of Nine Ball for two grand each way. The next evening we began our contest with the set of Nine Ball. I won that race, as I was supposed to do. Then we played the One Pocket match and I won that as well.

Bob and I were four grand up and flipping the coin for the next break. This was shaping up to be a great score. During the first match, all Bob did was sit up in the bleachers reading a book while I was down on the floor banging in the balls for thousands. Meanwhile this short, squat guy on the side lines with a big blonde beard, a red shirt and a beer belly, was getting real friendly.

This guy looked just like a big old bullfrog out squatting by the pond in overalls and a red shirt. He'd been acting like we were old friends. The whole time I was playing, he called me Danny and talked about road adventures he said we shared. I was drawing a complete blank on the guy and my memory was good, so my radar was on.

I won the flip for the next round of games and decided we would play One Pocket first. I was about ready to break off the first rack, when suddenly the doors in the back of the room exploded inward from the force of the jackboots hitting them. These guys could have just turned the knobs and walked in, but that would have lacked the drama they were seeking.

At first, I thought it was just the cops queering the action. But instead it was three guys wearing ski masks. When this sort of thing happens, your first reaction is that it isn't real, that it's just a dream and you're gonna wake up. But then you realize that this is very real and those are real guns and they actually are pointed at you and you could die. The result is an emotion like you've been hit with an intravenous lightening bolt.

It was a heist and these guys were ornery. If you want to get beat up, that's just fine with them. The armed madmen kicked people off stools and herded everyone into a corner of the room. It was as if they had been steered there. They picked out Eddie, Bob and me and brought us up front and made us strip naked.

In a few moments, we went from faces in the crowd to the stars of the show, standing there waving in the wind in front of maybe twenty guys, a couple of girls, and the banditos. They had the three of us lean against the wall with our hands supporting us. Then they came up from behind, and pistol-whipped us. When I got hit, I thought I was going out, but I fell to the floor and pretended to be out cold. Later, I learned that Bob had done the same thing.

But Burton was screaming for his life. I was scared he would spook them into shooting us all because he was freaking so bad. When they whipped him, they caught him on the side of the head and he was bleeding like crazy. I could feel his blood hitting my face and head and running down my neck.

Just as I thought maybe they were going to shoot us, one of them yelled: "Don't anybody move for twenty minutes." And the door slammed behind them. They left with our clothes and all our money. But at least we were alive.

We were stunned, catching our breath from fright. We had a moment of relief, when they burst back in the door. They had intended to leave in Bob's car, but it was one of those Ford Station Wagons that you had to pull back on the gearshift as you turned the key to get it started. Well, they couldn't figure that out. So here they were again, this time demanding how to start the car, and we were back at risk. Panicked bandits can make for a really bad day.

They screamed at Bob, "What's wrong with your fucking car, boy?" And Bob just lay there real still and said, "Nothing." Well, for some reason that seemed a good enough answer to them and they turned around and left.

About fifteen minutes later, someone in the crowd assumed that the crooks were gone and we could move. Bob and I were butt-naked, but at least we still had the grand of bank money back in the room. Somebody said: "Well, let's call the police and get 'em out here." That was about the last thing Bob and I needed, for the cops to start asking around about us and maybe find the wrapped cash in our room, so I said, "Why don't we not?"

It didn't take the crowd long to figure out that Bob and I had a reason not to report our loss and so one of them went and brought us some jeans so we could beat the authorities out of there and get back to our room. We went outside and Bob's car was still there with the key in it. We had a ride and knew the bandit trio had gathered no flashes of brilliance as concerned starting cars.

On the way back to the room, I looked in the back seat and there was one of the ski masks. For years, I kept that thing as a kind of sick souvenir. By the end of the night Bob, the ski mask and I were ensconced in another motel hundreds of miles away and safe from the jurisdiction of whatever sheriffs our lack of cooperation might have offended.

Next morning, Bob decided to call Eddie and see if he was okay. "They really pounded on him. He could be hurt bad." So he made the call and from what I overheard, I could tell that Eddie already had another stakehorse and wanted to meet us in Georgia for some more action. He wanted to win the money back, that the bandits had stolen.

When Bob hung up, he was smiling big. Here he had found good action where he thought there was none. We had already shown we had the best of Eddie, and here was Eddie begging for some more. We couldn't lose.

"Bob," I said, "when you phoned and asked me if I was on call I was—but not anymore. After that crap, I just want to go home and heal for a while." He drove me to the airport and that night I crawled into the cool of my own sheets. I was comfortable, safe and glad to be alive. Home felt good, but I knew what was coming. In a few days, the road would call again and my bed would seem like chains.

Chapter Sixteen
VEGAS LEADS ME BACK TO THE DOGS

The early eighties seemed quiet enough at the time, but events from then affected me much later. I met Geraldine, my current wife, in 1981, during a trip to Buffalo. My brother Joey had come to visit in Florida and he had a heart attack during the visit and died. My mom and dad were in a panic. They didn't know what to do in their grief. We had to get the body back to Buffalo where his wife and kids were, and he had a car in Florida, the one he used to get there. I arranged for the body to be flown to Buffalo for the funeral, and then I had to go back to Miami, get the car, and drive it up to his wife. I was going back and forth to Buffalo quite a few times during this period and sometimes I would kill a few hours in Buffalo at a friend's bowling alley and poolroom. I knew better, but my friend, a guy named Mike, finally talked me into running the place and staying in Buffalo again. Geraldine was one of the waitresses.

I had an apartment in Buffalo with a mirror over the bed and I was wild there. I had fallen entirely into the swinging bachelor lifestyle and I was having the time of my life. One girl got so jealous of my moves that she tried to shoot me, but she was a lousy shot. Mike finally decided that his best profit from the bowling alley could come from a fire, so the insurance company paid him off and I began plans to return to Florida.

This was where my problems began with the D.A.'s office in Buffalo. They figured I knew who torched the bowling alley and it

VEGAS LEADS ME BACK TO THE DOGS

really made them mad that I wouldn't tell them about it. But I was honest with them. "These guys are killers. If I tell you anything, I will die. So I'm not telling you anything." They never bought into that logic and this formed a grudge that would span twenty years.

I wouldn't rat out anyone, anyway. My father taught me from a young age to never be a fink. He always told me that if anything ever happened around me, that I never saw a thing. The lessons stuck.

But the D.A. kept bringing me into his office and they really wanted Mike. They told me, "Did you know that Mike tried to kill a federal agent?" And I said no, but this didn't pacify anything. I was mad at Mike myself—he burned down my livelihood, but I wouldn't squeal anyway. He was so disloyal to his friends that he took money out of my check every week for Social Security and taxes and stuff, but never deposited any of it. He just put it in his own pocket. When I went to collect on unemployment insurance after the fire, they told me I didn't have any because I had never worked anywhere!

When I found that out, I called Mike up and told him I was coming over to see him. I drove ninety miles an hour to get there and when I got there, he put his arm around me and gave me seven hundred to calm me down.

The D.A., Mr. Bruce, said he would send me to jail for not helping. So I left the interviews and went to Vegas. I got a call the next morning from a friend in Buffalo. "Mike's dead. Got his head blown off." Later, I found out that the FBI guy that Mike was supposedly going to kill had a big, framed picture in his living room of Mike with his head blown away by a shotgun. The death, a shotgun blast to the back of the head, was written off as a suicide.

ROAD PLAYER

In 1984, a friend of mine in Buffalo wanted to open a poolroom with me. But there was action in Detroit, so I told him to go ahead and do the initial planning and get the permits started and stuff and that I would be back from Detroit in a few weeks. In Detroit, which isn't far from Buffalo, Rosie was getting beat again. He would meet a group at the harness track in Northville. They would bet on the harness racing, then go across the street to a bowling alley and the group would dump some on Rosie there and then they would take him to the poolroom and they would dump him there.

When I got to town I wasn't able to enter the circle that got to play Rosie. In fact, I wasn't getting much action in Detroit at all. I turned fifty years old alone in my room while Grady Mathews got into action against Bugs, the great black player from Chicago. He played Bugs six consecutive nights and lost all six nights.

When I went into the Rack & Cue later that night, Grady was waiting for Bugs to arrive to play another set. Grady was a friend of mine, so I offered him this counsel:

"Y'know Grady, you've been losing every night to Bugs. You've got the right to ask for a ball or something. Bugs is a straight-up guy. He'll try you with a ball."

Grady never even considered my plan. "If I can't play someone straight up, I won't play them."

So I said, "Well then, do you mind if *I* ask him for a ball?"

And he said, "No, go right ahead."

When Bugs walked in with his backer, Cleveland Larry, I approached him and asked for some weight to play a bit of One Pocket.

Larry agreed to stake him to play me eight to seven. When I left that evening, I had won ten thousand from Bugs and that turned my depressing fiftieth birthday into a very happy one indeed.

What a room the Rack & Cue was. I was on my table playing a set for ten grand and a few tables over Rosie was playing for a hundred grand. Cash had a very short shelf life in the Rack & Cue. But action wasn't coming my way very easily, so in February I returned to Buffalo to open the poolroom. We called it Danny D's Classic Cue. Kelly Simpson came up to Buffalo and stayed with me, and we had a pretty cozy little existence there for the rest of the winter. Business in the room was very good and we stayed real busy.

But I became unhappy. I no longer belonged in Buffalo. Even though it was my home, I was no longer comfortable in the city. The winters that hadn't fazed me as a kid, now ripped through me. I hated having to go outside in the cold. My time in Florida had rid me of my cold hardiness. At the same time, I developed tumors in the colon and had to go to the Cleveland Clinic for treatment.

Kelly came with me to the clinic and was just wonderful. She stayed with me in the hospital for two weeks and got me through the ordeal. When I finally got out of the hospital, I felt good enough to play a little and Kelly mentioned a tournament in Madison, Wisconsin at Jerry Briesath's room. Jerry was one of the world's great billiard instructors and he ran his school out of his poolroom there, the Green Room, and held tournaments from time to time as well.

I had decided to move on and leave Buffalo, so I sold my end of the poolroom to my partner, and Kelly and I headed to Madison.

Kelly had said that after this tournament we should move out west. She said she had a little money and we could go to Las Vegas and she would open a poolroom there and take care of me until I was fully recovered from my illness.

One little problem Kelly and I had, was that we both had cars. She needed to fly out to Vegas to get things set up for us, so I had two cars to get from Buffalo to Madison and then out west. My buddy Barry Shaw did me the favor of coming and driving Kelly's car to Madison for me. But I still needed to get two cars from Wisconsin to Nevada.

On the first night of the tournament in Madison, I was late to the tournament room and missed the draw. When I came into the room, Mike Sigel came up to me with a big grin and said, "Danny, you got a really nice draw. I think you just drew yourself a nice tourney. You're stealing!" Actually, pool players don't like this news. It puts them off guard and they ease off the throttle too much. A lot of upsets come about because of easy draws.

My first match was against a fellow I had never heard of named Toby Dick. Toby won the lag, broke and made the nine-ball on the snap. He broke the next rack, made a ball, and then made the one-nine combination. This parade of easy games just kept on coming and before I could breathe, I was down eight to one and was looking around the room for Sigel. I wanted to hit him with something.

Toby Dick, my 'easy draw,' beat me nine games to one. As I sat in my chair collecting myself, my mind snapped to a time when Buddy Hall had a similar circumstance and it made me laugh. Buddy was playing in an event and he had the tournament all sewed up. He

VEGAS LEADS ME BACK TO THE DOGS

only had to get through a no-name guy to get to the final rounds and he was favored to beat everyone left in the tournament. He was on easy street.

The no-name guy had a streak of great luck. Every time he missed, Buddy wound up snookered. Buddy scratched on key balls. Buddy got beat and was sent over to the loser's side. No big deal, he would just have to play an extra couple of matches to get his win.

Buddy won his next match, as expected, but the no-name who had beaten him lost his next match, and got sent over to the one-loss side and Buddy had to play him again. Buddy was looking forward to the revenge. But the same thing happened again. Buddy couldn't ever get to the table with a shot and he got beat by the same guy again. No one had ever heard of this guy before or since, but Buddy will never forget his name. Whenever Buddy tells this story his biggest grin comes when he mentions the guy's name: "I was beaten by Delmar Schmeltzer."

My loss to Toby Dick set me up for an early departure from the charts. My mind was too much involved in what was going to happen in Las Vegas anyway, and on how I was going to get Kelly's car from Madison to the desert. I began asking around among the players looking for a driver. I figured I would pay their travel expenses and let them stay with us in Vegas a couple of weeks and have a good time as a payment for driving the car out there for me.

The only guy that wanted the deal was Louie Roberts. "St. Louis Louie" was well-known for his antics. Casual observers often thought he was crazy. His friends knew better, Many of us were concerned about how Louie abused himself with drugs and booze. At one tournament where he came in second, Louie got on the public address system and announced, "I'm a drug addict and an alcoholic and anyone in the room that wants the eight-ball for some serious money can have it." He was so feared at money matches that no one took him up on the offer.

Roberts said to me, "Danny, I love that drive. I haven't driven it in a while and I would really like to do it for you." I agreed because I had no other choice. I liked Louie; he was a heck of a fun guy. But I didn't relish the idea of turning over one of the cars to someone with his penchant for going off the edge. He could disappear with the car and that would mean that half of Kelly and my possessions would disappear as well.

I let Louie know of my apprehension. "No, Danny, don't worry! I'm all cleaned up now. I quit the drugs and stuff." I knew better. Louie might have wanted to quit that stuff, but he was much too addicted for me to believe that he was clean and would stay clean forever. He would backslide, and if he started slipping while in control of my wheels, I would have trouble. Louie had done some wild stuff to raise cash.

At a tournament in Nashville once, he showed up with absolutely not a dime. No money for the entry fee, no money for a hotel room, no money for food, nothing. So he walked in the room, found a spectator who liked his stick and sold him the cue for two hundred and fifty bucks. "You'll have to let me use the cue during the tournament, but as soon as play finishes, I'll give you the cue."

This gave him his entry fee. But he still needed a hotel and he still needed money for food and drink. So he sold the same cue to two other spectators with the same promise that they could take possession of it after the last match.

Roberts powered through the field. His game was truly one of the finest I have ever seen. In the finals, he dominated his opponent and was in the last rack when he remembered that three guys were all going to step forward at once to claim his cue when he sank the final nine. He lined up a shot on the five-ball in the side pocket and jawed it up. He feigned surprise first at the miss, then anger. He cursed loudly and swung the cue over his head like an axe and broke it over the rail of the table. The cue shattered into a pile of toothpicks.

His worries were over. He grabbed a house stick off the wall, won the tournament and left three shocked cue buyers speechless in their seats. They were so shocked, that they didn't even think to ask for their money back before he had time to get out the door.

So I was entrusting my car and belongings to someone who could, at any moment, just go off. The morning after the event in Madison, Louie and I were preparing to leave for our journey. "Louie, here's the deal. You stay behind me. Never pass me. And no booze, no drugs. Clear?"

"Yeah, Danny, no problem. I appreciate the drive. I'm ready."

For the first ninety minutes everything was fine. We were making good time, clipping away the miles and Louie was staying in my rear view just as promised. Then he suddenly passed me and pulled over, signaling me to stop. He got out, came to my window and said, "I'm falling asleep, Danny. I can't stay awake. I need something."

I reminded him of our 'no drugs' agreement. He said, "Let me just go into this place and get a cup of coffee and some No-Doz. That'll work." We went into the truck stop, he had his coffee and gobbled some No-Doz, and we continued our trip. Every hour or so, he would pull me over and complain of sleepiness and we would have to find coffee for him. At each of these stops, he would order a beer and I would have to be firm with him and tell him "no."

While I was sitting at the counter in these places, Louie would approach strangers and ask them for an upper. He thought he was fooling me, but I could hear him a couple of times and it was obvious that he was jonesing for a drug hit. The routine continued for four days. It was sometimes strained and often weird, with all the changes that Louie could go through in a day, but eventually we neared the Nevada line. Despite the problems that Louie presented, you just had to love him. He was a little kid at heart and relied on the drugs and the booze so much because he had a rough time in Vietnam. He was in one of the units that was sometimes targeted by children carrying hand grenades and such. The war made reality a desperate place for him, a place he avoided as often as he could.

When we crossed the border between Utah and Nevada, we pulled into a gas station and filled both of our tanks. I went inside to pay, and as the clerk was making my change I looked outside to see Louie pulling away fast. He had had all of my restraint he could handle and was escaping to freedom. In Kelly's car. With her possessions. Not that he was stealing anything. This was just the only vehicle available to him at the moment and it just happened to be full of her stuff. He needed to get out of there and he did.

VEGAS LEADS ME BACK TO THE DOGS

I had given Louie a hundred bucks to have in his pocket and he had plans for that hundred that didn't include me. I hauled out of the station and into my car as quickly as I could and sped off onto the Vegas highway in pursuit, but I couldn't catch him. Not knowing where he might stop, I had to pull into every little casino on the road and check the parking lots. I never found him on the highway, so when I got to Las Vegas I drove all over town looking for him.

Meanwhile, Kelly was spending time with her good friend, Mary Kenniston, waiting for me to get there. Mary had a poolroom in Vegas, Cuetopia, and I knew that Kelly would be there with her. When I got to Cuetopia, I told Kelly the story and we sat down and started calling all over town, putting out feelers for Louie. No one had seen him. I was a nervous wreck. I got back in my car, drove all the way back to the border again looking for him and then up and down the strip of Vegas, hunting everywhere. The next afternoon, I still hadn't seen hide nor hair of Louie and I called Cuetopia to check in with Kelly and she said, "We've got Louie. He's here with us."

"Is he all right?"

"Yeah, he's okay. He's all screwed up on something, but he's okay and the car and all the stuff is okay, too."

When I walked into Cuetopia and Louie saw me, he started begging me not to hit him. "I'm sorry Danny, I really am."

I went up to him, "Louie, I'm taking you to a hotel and I'm flying you back to St. Louis in the morning. I want you out of here."

Tony Banks was in the room and overheard the conversation and offered his assistance. "Danny, I'm staying in a motel right by the airport. I'll take him over there with me and I'll get him to the airport in the morning. There's no need for you to have to go all the way over there. You get some rest and I'll take care of Louie."

That sounded good to me, so I got some good rest that night for the first time in days, assured that Louie was taken care of and that that headache was on a flight out of town. But a few days went by and I got a phone call from St. Louis. It was Louie Roberts's sister. "What did you do to my brother?" she screamed, "he's in a room out there dying!" This came as a surprise to me, but she told me where he was and I went there.

When I went in, Louie was there with blood all over the room and running down his face. He had stumbled and torn himself up falling into table edges and doors. He was as messed up as a human could be. I called the airline and got him another reservation on the next flight to St. Louis and resolved that I would just stay with him and put him on the plane myself. In a couple of hours, he got hungry.

"You're supposed to feed me, Danny. I want to go out in the world with real people and eat at a restaurant." Rather than argue the logic of room service with him, I agreed and we headed out to a place to eat. When we got outside, he saw a security guard and started yelling, "This guy beat me up! You gotta help me! Look, I'm all bloody!"

After a long explanation to the security guard, we were free to go eat and I fed him and took him to the airport and put him on a plane. I can only imagine what his fellow passengers must have thought of this stumbling, bloody drunk as he weaved down the aisle to his seat. It must have been a very long flight for whoever was in the seat next to him.

VEGAS LEADS ME BACK TO THE DOGS

Things were back to normal now for me. Kelly found a house to rent and busied herself looking for a poolroom site. I tried to rest and get over the remnants of the colon treatments. One day I was in the house and I got a call from my old friend in New York, Barry Shaw. His dad owned some racehorses and he told me that one of those horses was running that day and that he liked the way this horse looked.

So I went down to one of the casinos and bet twenty bucks to win on it. The horse lost. That evening at the house, Kelly saw the twenty-dollar ticket sitting on the kitchen counter and blew a fuse. "I pay all the bills and you're blowing money on horses!"

I wasn't going to take that. "Wait a minute here, Kelly. This is my style. It's what I do. I bet on horses. I may be with you and you may be doing me a favor while I'm recuperating, but don't try to change me. That wasn't part of the deal! If that's what you need, then I'm outa here."

Well, that was a thought we agreed upon. I packed my bag and headed for the car. As I closed the trunk, I asked her how much she had spent since we were together. "Four thousand," she said. "Fine, I owe two thousand of that. I've got two hundred forty on me. Here's two hundred now, I owe you eighteen hundred." And I got in my Fiero with half a tank of gas and forty bucks and headed east. When I got out of the city and into the desert, I felt free again. Somewhat financially stretched, but free.

I headed the car towards Buffalo and stopped in every little bar and poolroom along the way; playing ten-dollar eight ball. By the

217

time I got to Buffalo, I had nine hundred dollars and Christmas had embraced the town with lights and carols.

After spending a nice holiday with my family, I headed south to Florida. I knew I could find the action there that I needed to stay solvent. Along the way, I made a stop in West Virginia. I won a couple of hundred in a room there and as I was leaving one of the patrons came up and told me about a room across town. "You could make a nice score there," he said.

So I headed across town and parked by the room he had told me about. Before I could reach the door, two heist men were on me with guns. I had been set up. These were novice heisters. Experienced thieves would have known to let me go in the bar and win some more money before taking me down, but these guys hit me on my way in. They took all my money, which I expected. But then they took my $3500 Szamboti cue stick. I pleaded with them. "Hey guys, don't take my tools. I know it's your job to rob folks and all, but my job is pool and I need my tools just like you need yours." They saw the logic in that and handed me back the cue.

I got back on the road, went to a pawnshop, and sold a stereo for a fifty dollar stake. I then slowly made my way to Florida playing small stakes pool all the way down the coast. When I got to Miami my wallet held about seven hundred bucks. No great wealth, but I could eat, afford a place to sleep, and I had the cash I needed to generate more cash.

It was January now and the Hollywood dog track was opening for the new season. I knew I could make some money there, especially if I could find a dog genius friend of mine, Adrian Megysiuk. He loved to play pool, but his calling was on the dog track. He knew the dogs better than anyone. Adrian had done me a great kindness once. When I was broke, he volunteered to spot me two bills. I really needed it and I thought the offer of two hundred was generous, When he handed me the money it was two thousand! So I knew I had a friend in Adrian, someone with whom I could work.

I went to the track and asked around and finally found someone who laughed at the name and said, "Oh, yeah, he's upstairs now." I went upstairs and Adrian greeted me with good news. "Danny, I've been here over a month watching the dogs. They've been doing the schooling races (workouts where eight dogs are put together and raced so they can get used to the track, the hardware and all the other little things that go on in a dog race) for the whole month and I took notes on every race. I know how these dogs all match up!"

The problem was that while he was ready to play, he had no funds with which to wager. "I can't get money from anybody. People have turned their back on me. Have you gotten a room yet?" When he discovered I hadn't, he insisted I stay with him.

He had a little house on Dixie Highway in Miami with fruit trees in the yard. There was no bed for me, so I slept on the couch. Adrian was so broke that there was nothing in the refrigerator, but vitamins and water. He ate fruit from the trees in his yard. That's how he was living. He ate off of his banana tree, his orange tree, etc. and that was all he was eating.

The next day we went back to the track and I gave him the seven hundred. "Here, play it." He liked a couple of dogs in the first two races, but they both lost. The next day, he liked three dogs all day and bet them. They all lost, too. On the third morning, we only had thirty dollars left. "Danny, I really like this one race and we will hit this race." So we put the thirty on this one dog and hit it for eighteen hundred bucks. We finally had a winner. Two races later he hit another one and we won another thirty-five hundred. This brought our total for the day to over five grand.

The next day he wanted to play the Super. "There's going to be over 80 grand in it and I think we can play it." So we did. We got nine live tickets. The way this worked was first you had to pick a trifecta and then you had to pick a superfecta. The trifecta means you have to pick the dogs one, two, and three in proper order. In the superfecta you have to pick the first four dogs to cross the wire, in proper order. You have to do both of these correctly to win and each day that no one wins, the pool rolls over and gets bigger.

He hit all nine live tickets on the trifecta, which meant we had nine tries at the Super and all that money. He keyed one of the dogs to win, another one to come in second, and scrambled four more dogs for third and fourth. The dog he picked for first jumped out to a five-length lead. The dog he picked for second trailed this dog but led the rest of the pack comfortably. The other dogs were positioned perfectly and sure enough, we hit that race and won eighty-four thousand dollars!

After that we couldn't lose. We won every night and soon had amassed a quarter of a million dollars in winnings. We were rich, but I was still sleeping on the sofa in a crazy man's house. One night, he woke me up in the middle of the night and commanded me into the kitchen where he had an orange on the table. He grabbed a broomstick, bent over the table cueing up on the orange and asked me how his stance looked. We had turned pocket change into fantastic money, but I had to get out of there.

I knew that the Rack 'Em Up Classic was coming up in South Carolina, so I took my money and said my goodbyes to Adrian and headed up the highway. When I got to the tournament, I saw Kelly across the room and still owed her eighteen hundred. I put the money in an envelope and handed it to her. She turned away with it, but came back a half hour later. "Did you make a score or something?"

"I made a lot of scores, Kelly, a lot of scores."

Chapter Seventeen
GUILT BY ASSOCIATION

From there I went back to Buffalo where a bus ran into my little Fiero and wrecked it. I bought a van and drove it out to Vegas where I was supposed to have a house to stay in with a friend. But he had left town, the house was a wreck, and I knew that I needed something else, another living arrangement. I called a friend in Phoenix who was about to open up the Golden Eight Ball. He said, "Come to Phoenix. You can be my house pro and you will do real well here." So I went to Phoenix. When I got there I helped him and Leonard Bludworth build a really great room. It had a table in the middle of the room sunken into a pit with seating all around so people could sit and look down on the games.

Business was huge from the very first day. We were open 24 hours a day and there was a constant waiting list. But the business created noise and the neighbors complained to the authorities. We built a wall around the place to appease the neighbors and reduce the noise. At first the bad guys would check their guns at the front desk when they came in, but finally we barred all firearms from the place. I led a team of really good bouncers and told them to handle all the problems internally. "Don't call the cops. You call the cops and you get a reputation as a trouble joint and then they'll be all over you. Don't call the cops for anything."

Eventually, two guys had an argument in the room and one of them pulled a gun. The other guy told him: "You better use that or I'll kill you." So he did. Shot him dead right there on the floor. And that spelled the end of the Golden Eight Ball.

But as long as it was open it was an action center for roadies. Ronnie Allen and I made a match there, where we each put up ten grand to play one set of One Pocket. Jay Helfert taped it and sold the tapes. Ronnie and I were to get fifteen percent of the sales every quarter. There were a lot of lies told about that match. It was absolutely a square deal and Ronnie had a flashback and beat me out of the money. Years went by without a quarter from Jay. Everywhere I went, people told me how much they enjoyed the tapes.

I called Jay about that once after a bunch of people told me how much they had enjoyed it. He said he had only sold sixty-two of them. I told him, "How odd, I must have met all sixty-two of them." He sent me a grand and that ended that.

But the match with Ronnie was a real highlight, even though I lost. For one, it was great action, with sweaters hanging over the rail and betting on every game. And Ronnie and I were pulling out shots that people had never even seen before. I won one game with a shot that can only be made on a wet table. On a dry table the shot will go long after the fourth rail and miss the pocket by a mile. But on a wet table it will shorten up and go.

The table in the Phoenix pit had become wet from all the bodies hanging over the rail, so when the shot came up, I called it and nobody could believe I would even attempt such a shot. It was the four-ball and it had to go four rails and into my pocket or I would risk selling out the game. The match was close at that point, so I sure didn't want to sell out. I guess I have to say that the shot just felt 'on.' Besides, it worked and really hit Ronnie like an uppercut.

After the Allen match-up, things kind of slowed down a bit for me on the One Pocket scene. But Nine Ball never slackened even a twit. Every road player worth his stake found their way to Phoenix and into the pit. CJ Wiley came to the Golden Eight Ball to play me once with his backer, Muscle John. This was not a pleasant visit. CJ had been going around the country taking on all comers and winning. He had just been out east and had given Johnny Archer the eight and robbed him. But he came to Phoenix at the wrong time. I was feeling good about myself and I was playing every day. Things were going great for me. I had a swimming pool in my backyard, I had action all the time and my game was as sharp as it had ever been.

CJ and Muscle John had a proposition for me. They wanted to play Nine Ball, race to twenty-one games, for five thousand per set with a guarantee of two sets. Someone would lose ten grand. When I won the first set, I began to flip a coin to determine the first breaker for the second set. "Wait, wait, wait," said Muscle John. "Let me talk to CJ for a minute."

So they talked. When they came back over Muscle John said, "We'll play you for five hundred a game." They wanted to change our deal. They didn't like the package they first came in with. I said, "Great! Just put up five thousand. I can't let you shoot at my five grand unless I'm shooting at yours." I wanted to see the money. I wasn't going to let them have a shot at what I had won unless I had an equal shot at them. For all I knew, they only had a few hundred dollars left between them.

When they declined to put up the five grand I told them again, "I'm not going to let you take a two-barrel shot at me." This was news they just didn't want to hear. It appeared to be particularly upsetting to CJ.

CJ started growling and puffing up at me. "I love pain. I love pain, I love pain," he said, maybe thinking that would get me to play on his terms.

I said, "You love pain? We'll get along great!! Cause I love inflicting it!" I continued. "You too, John. You guys are aggravating me. I'll go outside with both of you." They declined that offer as well and drove off into the heat.

Soon after that, the room was forced to close due to the murder and the continuing complaints from the neighborhood. When we shut down the Golden Eight Ball, I returned to Vegas. Throughout the late 80's, I lived there and everything was good. I made a fine living betting on the dogs and lived in a suburb supporting my wife, my daughter Jeanette and my mother-in-law. We were a happy family, secure in our lifestyle. When it fell apart, it crumbled very quickly.

I had become partners with some old friends from Buffalo in a poolroom in Las Vegas called Pool Sharks. When my partners sold it for over $280,000, I never got my end. My name wasn't on the papers because of the fear that my Italian name might prevent us from getting a gaming license for the slots and poker machines. So my old friends flipped me off and took all the money for themselves.

Then the casinos cut off my dog action. Dog racing in Vegas is not pari-mutuel—it is booked. So the casinos can lose on the bets. It's not just the betters setting the odds by how much money is put on which dog.

I had great success with the dogs and the casinos got tired of me beating them, so they finally cut me off. Some even refused to pay me my final winnings. The Horseshoe stalled me for days, before paying me my last winning ticket of $27,850. That would be the last ticket I ever cashed in that town. Suddenly, I was out of a way to make a living.

An old friend in Buffalo heard of my plight and called me. I had known Greg Hatch for decades, since school days, and we had been good friends. He told me to pack everything up and come to Buffalo. He said that my family could live with his family in their large home there. This turned out to be the worst favor anyone ever did for me. It nearly landed me in prison for life.

After we got to Buffalo and settled in, it became apparent that this was not a good situation. It looked like Greg was involved in moving cocaine around that part of the country, and while he never drew me into it, it was a bad situation and I didn't want to expose my family to a risk of that nature.

As soon as I could get a stake together, I moved the family to Florida. But the relationship with Greg, which I should have terminated, lingered. When he would come to Florida in the winter, he would stay with me and when I would go to Buffalo in the summer, I would stay with him. We would go to poolrooms together and scrape up action like the old days. This went on for around six years, both of us moving back and forth between Florida and Buffalo. We actually didn't spend all that much time together. He would spend a few weeks with me in the winter, and I would spend a few with him in the summer.

I kept my bass boat in Greg's garage and only used his house as a place to sleep. In the day, I was either bass fishing or at the track or in the poolroom, while he did his thing out of the house.

In 1999, I got a call from the Buffalo District Attorney, Mr. Bruce. He was still harboring a grudge about the bowling alley fire two decades previous. This was on a Thursday afternoon and they wanted me to come to Buffalo and talk to them on the next Tuesday. They said they had enough evidence on me to indict me for drug trafficking. Well, I knew I was innocent and I wanted to get this cleared up, so I got in the car and drove to Buffalo.

On Tuesday morning, I walked into the FBI offices in the Federal Building in Buffalo. We sat and talked for hours. They wanted to know what I knew about Greg's drug deals. But I really knew nothing at all. I had always kept that stuff at arm's length and purposefully stayed ignorant of what was going on. But they had him tied to another guy in Ft. Lauderdale and it was the Florida connection that put them on my tail.

Greg had called me one time and told me that there was a guy in Lauderdale that wanted to meet me. "He's a pool nut. You might wind up with a nice package from him for pool lessons or maybe sell him some cues. His name is Mark." So I called up this character and he came over to my house for breakfast the next day. We talked about lessons and he talked about staking me in some action games. He seemed a nice enough guy.

He was also betting football games across the country with Greg. When Greg won their bets, Mark would send him the money, no problem. But as time went by, Mark started winning the bets and suddenly, he couldn't get hold of Greg. Greg was hiding from him, playing dodge ball and avoiding the payoff. Mark tried to put me in the middle of it, calling me up and asking, "What's with your friend Hatch? When I was losing I paid him, but now I can't get paid. What's the deal with this guy?"

What I had no way of knowing then, was that these phone calls were being monitored by the FBI. They had the lines tapped. The FBI even had surveillance on me whenever I was in Buffalo. Which, as it turns out, was fine with me. All they could ever have seen me do was go fishing and mess with the boat.

Still, at the end of the interview, they took me down for booking. They fingerprinted and photographed me and I had to see a judge to find out what my bail would be. Not that it mattered. I was broke. When, as we walked by the cells, I returned an inmate's threat with the promise of knocking him out, the FBI man with me said, "Danny, we're not putting you in there, we'll go have breakfast and coffee and by then the judge will see you."

When I went before the judge, the FBI told him that they recommended I be released on my own recognizance. So I never did have to sit in a cell. And I went home for Christmas. As a condition of my release, I had to call a probation office in Ft. Lauderdale every day and if my number came up, I would have to go take a piss test for drugs. This continued for two years and it really hampered me.

I wasn't allowed to travel outside of Florida, so I had to turn down income opportunities—doing commentary for Accu-Stats and for giving out-of-state lessons. I used to go to France each year to coach their top players, but the travel ban knocked me out of that. It made life really tough.

At the end of the second year, I called my attorney. "Look, I've got an opportunity to go to Louisville and do some commentary there and I really need the money. Can you get me a pass out of this state for just a few days?" And he told me to go ahead and go. "They could care less where you go. Go to Derby City, have some fun, and make some money."

After I got back home, the Marshals arrested me for violating the terms of my bond. I had to go back to Buffalo to talk to the judge and I had to get there quick, with no money. So I drove to Buffalo again, met with my Public Defender, and he started telling me, "Danny, don't tell them I told you it was okay to go to Kentucky!" I never ratted out anyone, so I took the responsibility for everything.

The Judge pulled my bond and told the marshals to handcuff me and take me to jail to await trial. As they began to lead me away, my lawyer decided to do the right thing. He stood up and said, "Your Honor, it's not Diliberto's fault. He has complied perfectly with the rulings of this court. This was my fault. I told him to go to Kentucky." The Judge scolded me for protecting the lawyer and released me.

In July of 2001, I got word to come back to Buffalo for my trial. This time I took the Greyhound bus up the eastern seaboard to get there. When I got off the bus, I had ten bucks in my pocket and public opinion was I would be spending the rest of my life in prison. The prosecution, in the form of Mr. Bruce again, went for a tough jury. They knocked off all of the women, anyone with an Italian name, and anyone from the city. I had a jury of tough-minded rural white men. The prosecution had sixteen witnesses, thirteen of whom I had never even met. Under questioning from my lawyer, their witnesses admitted that they were all already in the pen and had deals to reduce their sentences in exchange for their testimony against me. But they really had nothing damaging to say. The only witness they had that could identify me admitted under cross-examination that she had been coached and shown my picture by the D.A.

This flipped the judge out. He emptied the courtroom and screamed at the prosecution that this looked like tampering and they had better straighten up. The trial lasted eight days with a parade of degenerates testifying as to Hatch's activities, but having no success at pinning me to the drug deals. One of them, Greg's nephew, testified that he had been given cameras and tape recorders by the FBI to entrap drug dealers in exchange for his own freedom. My lawyer asked him what he did with the equipment. "I sold it for crack."

At the end of the trial, my lawyer coached me as to how I should act when the jury came back in. "No emotion, Danny, no matter what they have to say." The jury deliberated for an hour and a half before coming back in and pronouncing me not guilty. What a relief. I remembered what my attorney had said and sat there stoic, but he broke down and was crying on my shoulder. The judge said, "Well, look at this! Diliberto's quiet and the lawyer's bawling." Then he turned to me and told me what I had waited so long to hear: that I was finally free again. I could go anywhere I wanted. So I went that day and crossed the border into Canada just because I could.

Next on my agenda in 2002 was an eye operation. For this I had to have a pre-op physical. When they gave me an electrocardiogram they found out that I had had a heart attack of which I was unaware. I think this happened during the stress of the trial. But it really shattered my feelings of indestructibility. I had managed to profit from ponies and dogs. I had thrived through fourteen prizefights and many more street fights, had challenged fate and luck on the road all those years, and now my heart was wearing out on me. I suddenly realized for the very first time that life didn't go on forever. My consolation is that at least it's too late to die young. I won.